MORE PLANTS LESS WASTE

MORE PLANTS LESS WASTE

PLANT-BASED RECIPES + ZERO WASTE LIFE HACKS WITH PURPOSE

MAX LA MANNA

yellow kite

First published in Great Britain in 2019 by Yellow Kite
An imprint of Hodder & Stoughton
An Hachette UK company
5

A CIP catalogue record for this title is available from the British Library

Hardback ISBN 978 1 529 39620 1
eBook ISBN 978 1 529 39471 9

Colour origination by Born Group
Printed and bound in Italy by L.E.G.O. Spa
Hodder & Stoughton policy is to use papers that are natural, renewable and recyclable products and made from wood grown in sustainable forests. The logging and manufacturing processes are expected to conform to the environmental regulations of the country of origin.

Yellow Kite
Hodder & Stoughton Ltd
Carmelite House
50 Victoria Embankment
London EC4Y 0DZ
www.yellowkitebooks.co.uk
www.hodder.co.uk

Editor: Lauren Whelan
Art direction and design: Hart Studio
Photographer: Andrew Burton
Food Stylist: Lou Kenny
Props Stylist: Louie Waller

CONTENTS

INTRODUCTION

MY STORY

Today, there are over 800 million people who are starving or don't have enough food to live an active lifestyle, but a third of food produced for human consumption is lost or wasted – that's 1.3 billion tons of food. This makes no sense whatsoever. After beginning my vegan journey in 2012, I started an online platform to reconnect people with their food and the planet in a positive, practical way. I've made it my mission to help turn the tide on plastic and breathe new energy into the leftovers that are typically destined for the bin and so far I've inspired thousands of people across the world to rethink their approach to consumption.

WHERE MY JOURNEY BEGAN . . .

I grew up in a large Italian–American household in small-town America. My passion for good food and protecting our planet stems from my parents: my father was a cook and owned restaurants, and my mother worked in television and was an avid gardener. Food and nature have always been a central part of our family life. I remember spending time in our garden with my mother, planting, watering and harvesting the produce we grew each season, from ripe red tomatoes and garlic, to leafy green lettuce and winter squash. I was lucky to have two parents who knew how to cook and who nourished our family with delicious home-cooked meals – we ate everything on our plates and never let leftovers go to waste. I loved a roasted chicken breast on the barbecue, my father's cheeseburgers, my mother's Saturday-night meatballs. We rarely went out to eat, we lived simply, enjoyed being around food and would all pitch in to help prepare dinner or wash up after a Sunday night feast.

My first job, aged 16, was a pizza dough boy and I have continued to work various jobs in the restaurant and food industry in some capacity ever since then. At the age of 20, I moved to New York alone to pursue my growing career in modelling – I was cleaning and bussing tables in the city between modelling jobs. But having grown up simply with family and food at the heart of my daily routine and having barely had so much as a drink before, the concrete jungle opened a door to a world I'd never seen. I lived life in the fast lane, caught up in the hustle and bustle of the city – I said yes to everything that came my way, with endless socialising, partying with supermodels and celebrities – and I quickly lost focus and sight of my health and what it meant to live well.

Struggling with direction and looking to start afresh, in 2016 I moved to Sydney, Australia, where I managed two restaurants and worked for an artisan vegan chocolate company. I realised that my health had taken a backseat and my love of cooking was dormant, but it was here that my passion for food was reignited and my journey to live in a way that felt kinder to the planet and my body began. Plant-based eating made so much sense to me and the more plants I ate, the better I felt.

Living in Sydney, I was suddenly surrounded by inspiring people doing exciting things to make a difference and it became so evident and clear to me that we live in a wasteful world and in turn, what a wasteful life I had been living. Each morning, I would take myself down to Bondi Beach and go for a run where I noticed people picking up plastic bottles and litter left by beachgoers. Despite finding myself in one of the most beautiful parts of the world, plastic and food waste still had a tight grip on consumers, yet there were people fighting to make a change. Feeling inspired by the sustainability wave I was seeing, I started to make changes to my own habits and choices. Each week I would go to the local farmers' market where everyone would bring their own reusable tote bags with them and they were riding bikes to get there. I started to bring my own bags with me and began carrying my own reusable water bottle. Some friends showed me a packaging-free store that allowed you to bring your own bags to refill your ingredients. It all made total sense. The less-waste lifestyle that I saw others living was looking very cool and accessible.

When I eventually made my way back to New York, I landed a bartending job at a trendy vegan/vegetarian restaurant in Manhattan. I wasn't cooking yet, but I pushed and challenged myself to learn as much as possible about food, drinks and the restaurant business itself. In a few short months, I managed to work my way up to cook with the other chefs. From being in a professional kitchen, I noticed that plant-based dishes and waste-free cooking seemed disconnected.

One evening on my way home from work, I met a man begging for food. Feeling helpless and wanting to do some good, I went home to see what I had to cook him a hot meal. There are moments that lead you to a new awakening and this was one of those occasions. I stared blankly at the rotting vegetables in my fridge, food that I had allowed to go to waste. The food I had spent money on would often end up in the bin because it had 'gone bad', or because I had cooked more than I needed. As I stared at the food I had to toss away something came over me. In that moment, I didn't just see wasted food, I saw wasted time, energy, water, resources,

labour and transportation as well as that starving man begging outside the train station.

As I started to learn about the environmental impacts of food waste and how I could do my bit at home, I simultaneously started to become more and more aware of the plastic packaging used for food and the pollution we create in our world. I decided that I was going to try and give up plastic and reduce my food waste for good. I started incorporating small changes into my daily routine, which eventually led to me starting to live a lifestyle called 'zero waste'.

My new approach to consumption was certainly not 'slow and steady' and at times this extreme overnight change posed some big challenges and led to struggles and plenty of failures. The goal and philosophy behind living zero waste is to send nothing to landfill. Is this possible? Is it even achievable? Through some difficult moments and breaking of old habits, I can tell you that yes, it is totally achievable. Today, if you can make one change, you are one step closer to living more sustainably and doing your bit to make the world a better, healthier place.

Our society is finally becoming aware of our destructive choices, from the plastic we consume, to eating meat at every meal. We are starting to understand that we need to consume consciously and this is what my book is here to encourage. MORE PLANTS LESS WASTE will be your go-to guide for learning how to shop, cook and live more sustainably.

I will share my favourite recipes, tips, tricks and hacks that will help make this both simple and enjoyable. I'll show you ways to upcycle your food scraps, such as how make a house cleaner using leftover citrus peel; how to waste less in the kitchen and use every part of your food – even the leftover water from tinned beans (which you can use to make butter) and I hope I'll inspire you to compost any scraps you can't use and grow your own herb garden on your kitchen windowsill.

I'll show you how to shop smart, how to be prepared when plastic tries to find its way into your life, how to say no to it (confidently) and how to cook easy and delicious plant-based meals with simple ingredients so that
you can discover a way of life with more purpose and less waste.

Every small change we make creates a bigger impact, so whether you decide to eat more plants or create less waste – or both, you are doing your best to protect and save our planet. Together, we can do this!

Max La Manna,
New York Chef and Sustainability Activist

WHERE'S ALL THAT FOOD GOING? FACTS YOU NEED TO KNOW ABOUT FOOD WASTE.

01. Food loss and waste amount to a major squandering of resources, including water, land, energy, labour and capital and needlessly produce greenhouse gas emissions. Food waste generates 3.3 billion tons of carbon dioxide, which accelerates global climate change.

02. If wasted food were a country, it would be the third largest producer of carbon dioxide in the world, after the United States and China.

03. If one quarter of the food currently lost or wasted could be saved, it would be enough to feed 870 million hungry people.

04. Eliminating global food waste would save 4.4 million tons of carbon dioxide a year, the equivalent of taking one in four cars off the road.

05. The average UK family is wasting nearly £60 a month by throwing away almost an entire meal a day.

06. In the UK, WRAP estimates that 8.3 million tons of food waste comes from consumers, 1.6 million tons from retailers, 4.1 million tons from food manufacturers, 3 million tons from restaurants and 3 million tons from other groups.

07. Globally, less than 3 per cent of food waste is recycled, which means food waste takes up more than 20 per cent of our landfills and incinerators.

LET'S TALK ABOUT PLASTIC

We made plastic. We depend on it. Now we are drowning in it. Plastic trash is littering the earth. Billions of tons of plastic have been made over the past decades. A mere 9 per cent of plastic is recycled, so what happens to the other 91 per cent? A new study estimates that roughly 12 billion metric tons of plastic waste will end up in landfills or natural environment by 2050: TIME IS UP! We need to act now!

» Each minute, 2 million plastics bags are being used around the world.

» The UK population throws away 295 billion pieces of plastic every year according to the Everyday Plastic Report.

'EVERY PIECE OF PLASTIC EVER CREATED STILL EXISTS TODAY'

» 500 million plastic straws are used in America every day; that's enough to circle the earth twice.

» Worldwide, this year over 5 trillion plastic bags will be consumed. That's 160,000 a second. Put one after another they would go around the world 7 times every hour and cover an area twice the size of France.

» Less than 1 per cent of plastic bags are recycled. They are most often made from polyethylene, which takes centuries to degrade. Each ton of recycled plastic bags saves the energy equivalent of 11 barrels of oil.

» At least 8 million tons of plastic enters the oceans each year. That's similar to emptying a garbage truck of plastic into an ocean every minute.

» Each year, 100,000 marine animals mistake plastic debris for food and die.

» If plastic had been invented when the Pilgrims sailed from Plymouth to North America – and the Mayflower had been stocked with bottled water and plastic-wrapped snacks – their plastic trash would likely still be around, four centuries later.

What we 'throw away' doesn't go away, it has to go somewhere!

Plastic is forever – is it time to rethink plastic?

WHAT I KEEP ON MY SHELVES

The pantry is the unsung (hero/heroine) of the kitchen. My cupboard is filled with glass jars and reusable containers filled with ingredients that I've sourced from bulk sections in various stores. The best way to ensure you cook delicious meals at any time is having a well-stocked pantry. It's also visually pleasing when you have a well-stocked shelf and easy to see what is running low and when you need to shop for more.

One way that I shop to ensure I'm not taking plastic into my home is in bulk – but of course I know that not everybody has this option. Every bulk store is going to have a variety of choices, so don't beat yourself up if you can't find a certain ingredient – just remember to bring your bags and containers with you.

PULSES

Typically, I love using dried legumes and beans and cooking them from scratch rather than using cans – it ensures I'm not creating any unnecessary waste from the can even though it can still be recycled. If you haven't tried this before I recommend soaking your beans overnight in a bowl of hot water and covering just before bed or for up to 24 hours, then follow my instructions on page 160 for how to cook them.

» Chickpeas
» Lentils
» Red kidney beans
» Haricot beans
» Pinto beans
» Black beans
» Cannellini beans
» Yellow split peas

KILNER
La Chinata

GRANOLA

GRAINS AND PASTA

Having a stock of grains and pasta is essential to creating delicious and simple meals. I always feel comfortable knowing that I have them on my shelf. Pair your grains and pasta with nuts, seeds and vegetables and you have a protein-rich meal.

All grains need to be washed before cooking so they are clean to cook with.

- Rice: short-grain, black and red rice
- Quinoa
- Rolled oats (you can also make an oat flour from them)
- Spelt
- Couscous
- Pasta (your favourites – any shape or size)

FLOURS AND BAKING ESSENTIALS

I have always loved baking and need to have a fully stocked shelf of flours and baking products – I never know when I'll have the urge to bake homemade bread or pancakes (see pages 180 and 42–5). Be sure to store flours in airtight containers, in a cool area on a dark shelf to maintain their quality and freshness.

- Plain flour (good for basically anything)
- Wholemeal flour (I change between plain flour and wholemeal)
- Spelt (makes delicious biscuits or bases for your homemade pizzas)
- Cornflour (this will always come in handy for thickening sauces and pie fillings)
- Bicarbonate of soda
- Baking powder
- Dried active yeast (I buy Fleischmann's in a jar)

NUTS AND SEEDS

Nuts and seeds always find their way into my cooking. Used whole they add depth of flavour and texture to your dishes, but you can also use them to create milks and cheeses. Store them in a dark place in your cupboard or fridge for protection and freshness.

- Almonds
- Cashews
- Walnuts
- Pecans
- Pistachios
- Coconut flakes
- Chia seeds
- Hemp seeds
- Buckwheat groats
- Sunflower seeds
- Pumpkin seeds

SWEETENERS

Missing something? Maybe it's some sweetness on your beautifully stocked pantry shelf. These come in handy for breakfasts and sweet dishes you may want to cook or bake, so have a well-stocked shelf and you'll be one happy chef. Here are a few sweeteners I like to use.

- Maple syrup
- Agave nectar
- Coconut nectar
- Brown rice syrup
- Dates or date sugar
- Brown sugar
- Coconut sugar

CONDIMENTS

Having a good supply of condiments is going to take your dishes to the next level. I love making my sauces from scratch, so if you can do that – amazing (and I've given you my recipes). If not, your bulk store or supermarket will most likely provide glass-packaged condiments.

- » Tahini (a great addition to dressings and hummus)
- » Tamari
- » Mustard (see page 190 for my recipe)
- » Ketchup (see page 191 for my recipe)
- » Mayonnaise (see page 191 for my recipe)
- » Nutritional yeast

SPICES AND HERBS

I'm all about the spice. Be sure to have a well-stocked spice pantry to provide amazing and delectable flavour to any of your dishes.

- » Cinnamon
- » Chilli flakes
- » Smoked paprika
- » Curry powder
- » Cumin
- » Coriander
- » Rosemary
- » Thyme
- » Basil
- » Oregano
- » Parsley
- » Black pepper
- » Pink Himalayan salt or sea salt

NOTES ON MY RECIPES BEFORE YOU GET STARTED

All the recipes in this book were made from and by plants. My hope is to open your mind towards eating more plants and creating less waste. As you read through the book, you will notice ingredients such as 'milk', 'cheese' and 'butter'. I've provided recipes for plant versions, however, if you want to use a non-plant alternative, feel free to do so – this is a judgement-free space.

I recommend and urge every one of you to try to source local, seasonal ingredients, plastic-free, where you can. However, I realise not everyone has access to a bulk store, farmers' market or their very own seasonal garden, so I encourage you just to do your best – make the appropriate decision and buy mindfully.

This cookbook isn't just another vegan cookbook – it's a cookbook to inspire you to make simple daily changes, to eat more plant-based, to live with less waste in your life. My meals are made and designed from food you probably already have sitting in your fridge, so I'd love you to use your own fridge as your starting point and not feel you have to follow a recipe to the letter. If you're already confident with your cooking try making swaps. If a recipe calls for kale, for example, and you don't have any, rather than going out and buying some, why not try swapping in spinach?

There are a lot of mixed opinions on the sustainability of certain ingredients, such as avocados, quinoa and almonds. Like everything we consume, these should be prepared and eaten mindfully and not to excess.

A FEW COOK'S NOTES

All fruit and vegetables are medium-sized unless otherwise stated.

All recipes use minimal equipment but you will need a blender and food processor to make some of the recipes in the book.

I normally use Maldon sea salt but there are several different types of salt out there for you to use. Use what you have in your cupboard before going out to buy a fancy new one.

Veg is never peeled unless otherwise stated and where it is I'll give you ideas for how to make use of the skins.

Nuts/herbs/tahini – often I haven't specified which type to use as I want to encourage you to use what you have in your kitchen.

Some recipes only serve two as this is a simple and effective way to cook less. If you're cooking for four then double up the quantities. Some recipes are larger portioned and if you have leftovers then you are in good hands because they store perfectly – either in the fridge or freezer – for you to enjoy them tomorrow or a day or two later.

MORE PLANTS LESS WASTE RECIPE ICONS

Throughout the book you'll see that some recipes are marked with icons; these are just some useful pointers for saving you some time, or helping you to save the planet.

ON THE GO

Don't have time to sit down at home to enjoy your breakfast? Need a packed lunch? These recipes sit well and travel easily in your reusable containers.

BEFORE BED

Start these recipes the night before – they work for you while you're asleep, saving you precious time come morning!

UPCYCLE

Let's not waste more than we have to. These recipes can be upcycled – use a can for projects at home or simply recycle responsibly.

LEFTOVERS

This icon is your guarantee that these recipes are delicious the next day, to make sure that nothing ever gets wasted.

FREEZER-FRIENDLY

These recipes can live in your freezer in a sealed container and are still as tasty when you come to eat them. Just be sure to heat your meal through thoroughly before digging in.

BULK COOK + STORE

These are some of my suggested staples to cook or create in double quantities and store in your leftover airtight jars for easy access when you need them!

01

MORE PLANTS BREAKFAST

SERVES 1–2, DEPENDING ON YOUR HUNGER LEVELS

POACHED BLUEBERRY ALMOND OVERNIGHT OATS

We made it – finally it's summer! Blueberries are in season and can be found at your local farmers' market but be sure to bring your own container with you to avoid any unnecessary packaging. Our mornings are short sometimes, so this is an easy and simple breakfast that you can begin the night before. Take this on the go or enjoy at home with your lover or kids to start your day off right.

100g rolled oats
1 tbsp chia seeds
pinch of salt
½ tsp vanilla extract
200ml milk (I like oat; see page 194 for how to make your own)
90g blueberries, plus extra for topping
2 tsp maple syrup
2 tbsp whole almonds, chopped
120ml cashew yoghurt (see page 38 for how to make your own)

Put your oats, chia seeds, salt, vanilla and milk into a bowl. Give it a good stir and cover. Place the bowl in the fridge overnight.

The next morning, place the blueberries and maple syrup in a small saucepan over a medium–low heat for about 3 minutes, stirring occasionally, until they start to burst and pop, then remove from the heat. At the same time, add your chopped almonds to a pan and toast them over a medium heat for 3 minutes as well.

To serve, divide the oats between two bowls (unless you're hungry), add a spoonful of cashew yoghurt, the poached blueberries and toasted almonds. Or if you're taking them on the go, pour them into a reusable glass jar.

SERVES 2–3

ORANGE, HAZELNUT AND COCONUT BIRCHER MUESLI

Growing up I never had Bircher muesli, but since arriving in the UK, I've discovered this healthy and hearty goodness and I can't get enough of it. Seriously, it's something I'd love to eat every day. This is an easy, make-ahead breakfast.

Toasting hazelnuts and almonds ups their flavour profile and the freshly squeezed orange juice adds an uplifting zing.

75g almonds
75g hazelnuts
250ml cashew yoghurt (see page 38 for how to make your own) or coconut yoghurt
grated zest and juice of ½ orange*
120g rolled oats
75g desiccated coconut
1 tsp vanilla extract
2 apples, finely grated

To serve
orange segments
extra yoghurt

Preheat your oven to 180°C. Once hot, spread the nuts out on a tray and toast for 8–10 minutes, or until lightly browned. Store in an airtight container.

In a large mixing bowl stir together the yoghurt, orange zest and juice. Add the oats and allow to soak overnight. In the morning, remove from the fridge and add the coconut, most of the toasted nuts and the vanilla and mix well.

To serve, stir through most of the grated apple, then spoon into bowls and top with orange segments, extra yoghurt, grated apple and additional toasted nuts.

The Bircher without apple added can be stored in the fridge up to 3 days.

TIP

Store the leftover orange peels to make a Citrus Bomb house cleaner (see page 125)

MAKES ABOUT 500G

BANANA BREAD GRANOLA

It breaks my heart to see bananas ending up in the bin, they are the perfect example of mistreated fruit and the number one wasted fruit crop in the world. Over a hundred million tons of bananas are discarded in factories before they even reach our supermarkets due to their 'undesirable' wonky, imperfect shape; if one banana in the bunch is too small or shaped differently – the whole bunch is thrown away. Let's not add to this devastating statistic – there are so many opportunities to utilise this amazing fruit. My crunchy, nutty granola will make your home smell like banana bread! What more could you want?

300g rolled oats
½ tsp ground cinnamon
2 tbsp brown sugar or coconut sugar
½ tsp salt
1 tbsp shelled hemp seeds
100g pecans, roughly chopped
100g walnuts, roughly chopped
40ml coconut oil
60ml maple syrup or coconut nectar
1 tsp vanilla extract
2 ripe bananas

Preheat your oven to 180°C. Mix the oats, cinnamon, sugar, salt, hemp seeds and nuts in a large bowl.

Put your coconut oil, maple syrup and vanilla into a small saucepan over a low heat and mix until the oil has melted.

Pour the melted oil mix into a mixing bowl and add the bananas. Smash the banana with a fork or hand blender until very slightly chunky. Next, combine your wet and dry ingredients and mix well.

Spread the mixture evenly over a baking sheet – make sure it doesn't get crowded; you may need to use another baking sheet. Bake for 15–20 minutes until golden brown. If you need more time bake for another 5 minutes, or until crisp.

Remove from the oven and toss the granola a bit to release a bit of heat. Allow it to completely cool on the baking sheet. Store in a sealed container or Mason jar – it should keep for a couple weeks.

TIP

If you like clumpy and crispy granola, which is my personal favourite, do not touch the granola while it bakes. If you want crumbly granola, toss and stir a bit during the process.

MAKES 500ML

EASY CASHEW YOGHURT

Do you ever think how your great-grandparents used to cook? They would have created dishes from scratch, without relying on products bought in ready-made plastic that we are all too familiar with now. Yoghurt for me is easy to make and reminds me that good things take time, maybe two days in this case. This yoghurt is great with granola, for thickening smoothies, on top of curries and so much more.

- 200g raw cashews, soaked for at least 4 hours or overnight
- 250ml filtered water
- 2 tbsp maple syrup
- 1 tbsp vanilla extract
- pinch of salt
- ⅓ tsp probiotic powder or 2 capsules (reuse the bottle for on-the-go dressings #upcycle)

Drain and rinse the soaked cashews and add them to a blender or food processor along with the other ingredients and blend on a high speed for 3–5 minutes until the mixture is completely smooth and silky.

Transfer to a deep bowl and cover with a clean towel or muslin cloth. Keep in a warm and dark place (I like using my kitchen cupboard) for between 24 and 48 hours, depending on how tangy you want it. It will be ready once the mixture looks foamy and has a tangy scent. When the yoghurt has fermented – give it a good stir and transfer it to a clean jar. Simply refrigerate to thicken and then enjoy – it's good kept in the fridge for up to a week.

TIP

Every instrument used for making this should be very clean – you don't want to be growing the wrong thing!

JAN/2022
90042

SERVES 2

GOLDEN MILK PORRIDGE

I had an epiphany over a bowl of porridge. I'd never been one for porridge until I tasted this one. I had just moved to Los Angeles and was partying with some friends at their house on Venice Beach. I ended up spending the night and woke up to a delicious smell – my friend's mother was stirring a massive pot of porridge. I had never tasted anything so profoundly comforting in my life.

She never shared her recipe with me, so for the next year I ate porridge for breakfast in pursuit of finding that deliciousness. It took me over a year to figure it out but I'm happy to share it with you now.

For the golden milk

370ml milk of your choice

½ tsp turmeric (ground or freshly grated)

¼ tsp ginger (ground or freshly grated)

¼ tsp ground cinnamon

pinch of black pepper

pinch of salt, plus extra to serve

pinch of vanilla bean (paste or extract)

½ tsp maple syrup (or coconut sugar), plus extra to serve

For the oats

1 tsp coconut oil

100g jumbo oats

2 chopped and frozen bananas

handful of golden raisins

1 tbsp chia seeds

1 tbsp shelled hemp seeds

To serve

almond butter

berries

Begin by making your golden milk. Pour the milk into a small saucepan over a low heat, add the rest of the ingredients and whisk well for 1 minute. Once the liquid starts bubbling around the edges, remove it from the heat and leave it to sit.

In a pan, melt your coconut oil over a low heat, then add the oats and frozen bananas and mix. Add the golden milk and stir well, then add the golden raisins and seeds. Keeping the heat low, continue to stir until the consistency is to your liking, then remove from the heat and serve with a spoonful of almond butter, fresh berries, an extra drizzle of maple syrup and a pinch of salt. Namaste.

MAKES 8–10

ONE-BOWL BANANA BUCKWHEAT PANCAKES

These pancakes are life-changing. Remember the convenience of instant pancake mix where you just add water? This is the zero-waste version of that, but much fluffier and definitely more delicious. And they make use of those bananas that are getting spottier by the second. A perfect weekend breakfast.

1 medium ripe banana (brown and spotty is better)
25ml oil, plus a little extra to grease the pan (I like coconut)
25ml maple syrup (any liquid sweetener will work)
2 tsp baking powder
¼ tsp salt
240–300ml milk (see page 194 for how to make your own)
280g flour (I like half oat, and half buckwheat)
45g dark chocolate chips (optional)
handful of fresh berries (optional; frozen work too)

To serve (optional)

aquafaba butter (see page 178), fruit, nuts, seeds, nut butter, maple syrup

In a bowl, mash the banana. Add the oil, maple syrup, baking powder and salt and whisk to combine. Add the milk slowly and mix (add more milk to your liking).

Add your flour to the bowl and mix – be careful to not mix too much. You are aiming for a thick but pourable consistency. If it's too dry and not scoopable, add a splash of milk to loosen it; if it's too wet, add a small amount of flour. You want your batter to be thick, but pourable. Feeling adventurous? Add the chocolate chips or berries now and gently fold them into the mixture.

Heat a non-stick frying pan over a medium–low heat. Once ready, pour your desired amount of batter into the heated pan and repeat according to how many you can fit in your frying pan. The batter will begin to bubble and the edges will appear to be drying after about 1–2 minutes. Next, carefully flip the pancakes and cook until browned on the underside. Transfer the pancakes to a plate and cover with a tea towel to keep warm until serving.

Serve each stack as you like – perhaps with a light spread of butter, fresh fruit, chopped nuts and seeds, maybe even some nut butter and maple syrup. Have fun!

MAKES 6–8

LEMON BLUEBERRY AND COCONUT PANCAKES

'I love cleaning up the kitchen after I've made pancakes,' said no one, ever. These pancakes are a one-bowl magic trick in your kitchen. Pour, mix, cook, serve, eat, done. Want a pancake that is pillowy, fluffy, and perfectly sweet? Look no further.

170g plain flour (wholewheat, optional)

30g coconut flour (buckwheat flour, optional)

1 tsp baking powder

grated zest of ½ lemon

2 tbsp desiccated coconut

260ml milk (I like almond or oat milk, see page 194 for how to make your own)

80g blueberries

1 tbsp coconut oil, melted, plus optional extra for frying

To serve

nut butter

crushed nuts

shelled hemp seeds

maple syrup or agave nectar

Put all the dry ingredients, including the lemon zest and coconut, into a bowl and mix well. Next, add the milk, blueberries and coconut oil to the dry ingredients. with a spoon, lightly stir your mixture to create a batter. You are aiming for a thick but pourable mixture. If it's too dry and not scoopable, add a splash of milk to loosen it; if it's too wet, add a small amount of flour.

Once the batter is a perfect consistency, heat a non-stick frying pan over a medium heat. If your frying pan is well seasoned you won't need to add oil – if not, add a small drop of oil and tilt the pan to let it coat the surface of your frying pan evenly.

Add a big spoonful of batter to the heated frying pan and gently spread into a small disc; repeat for as many pancakes as your frying pan can fit. Cook for 1–2 minutes, or until bubbles form on the exposed surface and the underside is golden brown. Flip the pancake(s) and cook for 1 minute, or until golden brown. Stack your cooked pancakes on a plate and cover with a tea towel to keep them warm while you cook the rest.

Serve your pancakes with nut butter, crushed nuts, hemp seeds and a generous pour of maple syrup or agave nectar.

MAKES 10–12 MEDIUM FRITTERS

SPRING VEGETABLE AND HERB STEM FRITTERS

I love it when the seasons change and there's an abundance of new produce. I prefer to eat seasonally and locally where possible, because it's a way for me to feel closer to the root of things, which is important as a city dweller and sustainability advocate.

5 asparagus stalks, grated
2 carrots, grated
2 large new potatoes, peeled and grated (keep the peel aside for later)
1 small red onion, diced
120g cheese (optional; use any kind you like – if you have it in your fridge)
1 red chilli, deseeded and thinly sliced
handful of fresh dill, chopped (reserve a bit for garnishing)
handful of fresh parsley, chopped (reserve a bit for garnishing)
½ tsp coarse sea salt
25g ground flaxseed/ psyllium husks, chia seeds or flaxseed (optional)
60g chickpea, oat, plain or buckwheat flour
100ml milk or water
extra virgin olive oil, for frying

To serve

beetroot hummus (see page 84) or coconut yoghurt
chopped herbs

Place your grated asparagus, carrots and new potatoes in a bowl, then take a tea towel and press your vegetables to remove any excess liquid.

Add all the remaining ingredients to the bowl and mix until everything is evenly combined.

Place a frying pan over a medium heat with a light drizzle of extra virgin olive oil. Bring the heat to medium–high. Using your hands divide the mixture into about 10–12 rough balls, then press each one together with both hands to bind and flatten slightly to make small fritter shapes.

Placing a few in the frying pan and cook for about 3–5 minutes, or until lightly golden brown around edges. Flip and repeat. Serve alone or with leftover beetroot hummus or coconut yoghurt – finished with freshly chopped herbs.

TIP

Have any leftover fritters for lunch the next day or freeze them for up to 2 weeks.

CREATING LESS WASTE – A MINDSET FOR THE FUTURE

I'll never ask you to go completely zero waste, but I will ask you to start minimising and creating less waste. These micro changes that I use in my daily life truly do make a difference – start now and your planet will thank you later!

01. Swap plastic bags for reusable bags. Bring them with you wherever you go to ensure you're not using plastic unnecessarily.

02. Always have a reusable water bottle with you – 1 million plastic bottles are purchased every 60 seconds and 91 per cent of all plastic is not recycled.

03. Incorporate taking your reusable container, cutlery and cloth as a napkin with you as part of your routine when you leave your home each day.

I bring a stainless steel container (any type of container can work), bamboo utensils or the cutlery in my kitchen drawer wrapped in a linen napkin – open up an easy route to saying no to plastic when you're in a rush!

04. Buy more whole foods in less packaging. Let's face it, most of our supermarkets are just littered with plastic and most of our food is covered with it too. This can be challenging for some because we are told that purchasing food in plastic packaging is the healthier option and helps preserve our food for longer but it is not completely true. If you have the choice to choose a plastic-wrapped banana or natural bananas without plastic – what would you choose? Hint: bananas already have their own natural packaging, so why do we need plastic? Becoming aware of the choices we make is the first step to creating less waste. Wouldn't you want the whole orange rather than segments sold to you in a plastic container?

05. Make tasty dishes at home. The restaurant industry is another huge contributor to all things waste. Cooking your own meal from scratch or assembling leftovers from the fridge will not only save you money, but tends to be healthier for you and the planet.

06. Make your own beauty products and home-care products from natural ingredients – you may already have all the ingredients you need in your cupboard at this exact moment. If we're conscious of the food we put into our bodies, what about what we put on and around our bodies? Taking care of our health isn't just about the food we need for our body, it's also what we use on our body and in our home environments.

07. Buy clothes second-hand. The fashion industry is one of the largest contributors to waste, through water and energy waste, not to mention its unethical labour practices and the amount of carbon emissions generated when a piece of clothing is not cherished or valued and sent to landfill. Enjoy the pieces you own already and if they break – fix them!

SERVES 2–3

DO IT YOURSELF BAKED BEANS ON TOAST

I'm aware that beans on toast is something of a British staple, so this one goes out to all my UK homies. A lot of canned products are heavy in salt and often contain preservatives and additives (such as BPA). Cooking your own beans is definitely healthier and will work out cheaper if you make them in bulk. They're simple, delicious and perfect for a lazy Sunday breakfast (in bed . . .).

- 2 tbsp olive oil
- ½ onion, diced
- 2 garlic cloves, chopped
- ¼ tsp chilli flakes
- 1 tsp smoked paprika
- 400g tomatoes (fresh or canned, see how to upcycle your cans on page 200)
- 1 tbsp tamari
- 3 tbsp apple cider vinegar
- 120g mushrooms (any variety), diced
- 2 tbsp brown sugar or maple syrup
- 2 x 400g cans pinto beans, drained and rinsed
- 4–6 thick slices of bread
- aquafaba butter (see page 178), olive oil or avocado
- fresh coriander, to garnish (optional)

Put a large saucepan over a medium–high heat. Add the oil, onion, garlic, chilli flakes and paprika. Stir occasionally until the onions are translucent and the garlic begins to brown lightly.

While you wait, blend the tomatoes, tamari and apple cider vinegar until completely smooth. Add your mushrooms to the saucepan and stir well. Reduce the heat, then add your puréed tomato mixture. Add the brown sugar and stir for 2–3 minutes. Fold in the beans and stir well for 3–5 minutes over a low heat until the mixture thickens a little.

Toast your bread and spread it with aquafaba butter, olive oil or avocado. Add heaped spoonfuls of the beans – if you have coriander laying around, chop finely and sprinkle it over for the final touch. I've heard that the Great British among you also like a smattering of cheese atop your beans, in which case please refer to my cheese recipe on page 179. Store leftovers in a sealed container in the fridge and reheat to serve – maybe take to work or have leftovers for dinner.

MAKES 2 PLENTIFUL BOWLS

PLASTIC-FREE TOFU SCRAMBLE BREAKFAST BOWL

As a teenager, my father would take me to a diner every day for hash browns and scrambled eggs before school. Thanks Dad! Thankfully, this recipe means I can satisfy my nostalgic craving – with more plants. But wait, isn't tofu packaged in plastic? Yes, it is the majority of the time, but there are ways to acquire package-free tofu.

Step one: have a reusable container with you and you're halfway there. Most Asian supermarkets will have tofu displayed behind the counter – simply ask for your desired quantity and hand over your reusable container. Done!

1 block of firm tofu (about 280g), drained

100g quinoa

1 large sweet potato, grated (keep the skin on)

1 tbsp flour

1 tsp smoked paprika

pinch of dried herbs (optional)

rapeseed oil, for frying

1 garlic clove, chopped or crushed

50g tomato, diced

½ tsp ground turmeric (fresh and grated works wonders too)

2 handfuls of spinach, (or finely chopped kale, swiss chard, or rocket)

herbs (I like dill, coriander or parsley), finely chopped (optional)

1 avocado (optional)

salt and pepper

For the avocado sauce (optional)

1 avocado

splash of apple cider vinegar

a few coriander leaves and stems

pinch of dried parsley

splash of water or oat milk

Press the tofu with a tea towel to remove excess water. Cut the tofu into 2cm cubes and set aside.

If you are making the avocado sauce, blend the avocado with the other ingredients and a pinch of salt and pepper.

Place the quinoa in a medium saucepan and turn the heat to high. Toast the quinoa for 1–2 minutes before adding 150ml cold water. Stir well and bring to the boil. Once at a boil, reduce the heat to low, cover and cook until fluffy and light.

To make the hash browns, begin by grating the potato using the large holes on your grater. Press and dry the potato using a tea towel to remove any excess water.

In a bowl, mix the grated potato, flour, paprika, some salt and pepper and maybe a pinch of dried herbs, if you like. The sweet potato mixture should be wet but still hold together as a batter.

Add 2 tablespoons of oil to a frying pan. Bring it to a medium–high heat, where it's not overheating or smoking. Take 2 spoonfuls of

the sweet potato mixture and roll it in your hands to bind, then press it gently with your palms to create a smaller, slightly thinner patty – you should get about six or seven from the mixture. Add a few patties to the frying pan, keeping them spaced apart and not overcrowding the pan. After 3–4 minutes, the potato should be crispy and golden brown around the edges. Flip and cook for another 3–4 minutes on the other side. To keep your hash browns warm, place on a plate and wrap with a tea towel to retain the heat while you cook the remainder.

Once all the patties are cooked, put the same frying pan on a medium–high heat and add a teaspoon of oil. Next, toss in the garlic and fry until lightly brown. Lightly fold in your cubed tofu and fry for 4–5 minutes. With a spatula or wooden spoon, begin to break up the tofu to give it the 'scrambled' texture. Toss the tomato and turmeric into the pan and mix well, then reduce the heat, cook for 1 minute then remove from heat.

To serve, divide the spinach between two bowls. Add a generous spoonful of your fluffy and light quinoa, hash browns, scrambled tofu and freshly chopped herbs. Serve witheither sliced avocado, or pour over the avocado sauce. Any leftover hash browns can be kept in the fridge and eaten for breakfast or lunch the next day.

SERVES 2

IMMUNITY-BOOSTING ORANGE RASPBERRY SMOOTHIE

For the red layer

150ml milk (see page 194 for how to make your own)

50g strawberries

50g raspberries

30g beetroot (leftover; optional)

For the orange layer

150ml milk (see page 194 for how to make your own)

1 orange, peeled and sliced (keep the peel and see pages 125 and 202–3 for how to use them)

1 banana, frozen

¼ tsp grated ginger

¼ tsp ground or freshly grated turmeric

To serve

2 tbsp granola (see page 36)

I try to hydrate as much as I can when I wake up in the morning, starting with 1–2 litres of water. I don't drink coffee but I love the energy that a nutrient-dense smoothie gives me. Fresh fruit like raspberries and strawberries can be found at the farmers' market during spring and summer months (depending on where you live). Just be sure to bring your own container or bag, so the farmer can reuse the container they come in.

Put the red layer ingredients into a high-speed blender and blend until smooth. Divide between two glasses. Rinse out the blender, then add your orange layer ingredients and blend again. Slowly pour the orange over the red layer.

TIP

To have beautiful separation of colour, pour slowly and close to the glass. We eat with our eyes too! Sprinkle a bit of granola, nuts or seeds on top to give it more oomph.

SERVES 2

DON'T WASTE YOUR GREENS SMOOTHIE

I'm no doctor, but you can't argue with the power of dark leafy greens, which are also referred to as 'DLGs' in my household. I like to freeze my DLGs of choice (spinach, kale, Swiss chard), so I'm always prepared to get my super green smoothie hit in a hurry. Not only does the freezing process save them from going to waste if they're soon to go off, it also retains the nutrient density of the produce.

- 300ml milk (of your choice; see page 194 for how to make your own)
- 1 banana, frozen
- ½ cucumber (can be frozen)
- ½ courgette (can be frozen)
- 90g blueberries (can be frozen)
- 20g dark leafy greens (spinach, kale, Swiss chard)
- 1 tbsp hemp or chia seeds
- 1 tbsp nut butter (of your choice)
- 1 tbsp protein powder (optional)

To serve:

- granola (see page 36 for how to make your own)
- fresh berries

Pour your milk into the blender first, then add all the remaining ingredients. Blend until smooth and creamy. If you want added protein, add a scoop of your favourite protein powder or add more leafy greens.

Drink immediately or take with you in your reusable container. Serve with crunchy granola and fresh berries.

HOW TO COMPOST

When I started looking at ways to reduce my environmental impact, there was one form of action that stood out from the rest, and that was composting. In my opinion, it's the greatest thing we can do for our planet.

Do you know where your wasted and uneaten food go? Landfill.

This is extremely harmful to our environment as the food breaks down and generates and releases methane into our atmosphere, making it harder for us to breathe and warming our planet. Our ignorance about disposing our food properly is driving us straight towards climate change.

Don't worry because it's not too late to start composting your unwanted food scraps and waste. Learning what compost is and how you can easily start today is the first step.

WHAT IS COMPOST?

'Compost is organic material that can be added to soil to help plants grow', according to the US Environmental Protection Agency. Composting is the natural process whereby organic material breaks down into a nutrient-rich soil that can be used in your garden as a fertiliser. That means bigger produce, prettier flowers and a healthier garden can come at no extra cost to you once you start saving your food scraps and turning them into 'plant food'.

More and more people are becoming interested in embracing this sustainable practice and creating their own compost heap at home by recycling the food waste and scraps that would normally just be thrown away. Being more mindful about food waste is leading to a composting revolution! Are you ready to get involved?

WHY DOES IT BENEFIT THE ENVIRONMENT?

The process of composting is hugely beneficial to the environment, not only because it reduces the amount of food and garden waste sent to landfill, which in turn reduces the amount of methane greenhouse gas, but it's also a crucial part of the nitrogen cycle. The plants we eat need nitrogen-rich soil to grow and build protein and soil from a compost heap is one of the most natural ways to achieve this. By returning your food waste to a compost heap and not putting it in a plastic bag in your kitchen that is sent off to landfill, you will ensure that your soil (our soil) is receiving nutrients to create a healthy environment to grow more food.

HOW TO COMPOST AT HOME

When I started composting and rethinking my food waste, I thought it would be a difficult task but in fact it's simple.

Typically, you want to have an outdoor space for your compost and a closed bin will keep the smell and animals away. Take an empty container – something you may find at a hardware store or your local gardening shop, but something that is big enough to hold your food waste. Depending on where you live you may need to protect your compost pile with a fence or what I've done is place a heavy rock on the lid so no animal can get in.

Here comes the magic, for a healthy compost you are aiming for equal parts green and brown material. The brown material contains carbon which feed the organisms that break down the scraps and the green material provides the nitrogen that is vital for structuring your new soil. Next, your soil needs oxygen and water. Without air, your pile will rot and smell, so poke a few holes around the bin or keep the lid ajar. The water keeps the soil moist and helps break down the material. Sprinkle your compost with a bit of water every week or so – it should be moist like a towel you've just wrung out.

Turn your compost every few days so that the air can penetrate.

If you don't have the space to start your own at-home compost outside, don't worry, there's still a simple option to save those scraps! Many local councils can now provide you with a small kitchen caddy or general food waste bin and offer a collection service at the same time as your other recycling.

DO COMPOST		DO NOT COMPOST
BROWN WASTE	GREEN WASTE	
Most sawdust	Tea bags	Dirt/soil
Chopped woody prunings	Citrus peel	Ashes from a stove, fireplace, or barbecue
Pine needles	Coffee grounds	Animal products (meat, bones, fish, grease/fat)
Fallen/dried leaves	Coffee filters	Dairy products
Dried grass	Shrub and grass clippings	Sawdust from plywood/treated wood
Straw	Fruit waste	Diseased plants
Shredded paper/cardboard/newspaper	Vegetable waste	Seed-bearing weeds
Soil from used flower pots	Wilted flowers	Manure or human waste
	Young weeds	

02

WASTE NOT LUNCH

SERVES 6

AVOCADO BUTTER LETTUCE CUPS

2 large sweet potatoes, peeled and cut into 1cm cubes (see page 103 for how to make crisps from the skins)

extra virgin olive oil, for drizzling

100g dried chickpeas (soaked overnight and cooked, see page 160, or 200g if using canned)

1 head of butter lettuce (or cabbage)

3 avocados, thinly sliced

175g cherry tomatoes, halved

1 cucumber, cut into half-moon slices

30g pumpkin or sunflower seeds, toasted in a dry pan

small bunch of coriander, roughly chopped

grated zest and juice of 2 limes

pear slices (optional)

salt and pepper

This is an all-time favourite for me, and soon to be for you too (I hope). The great thing about this meal is that it can be enjoyed as a light lunch or shared as a summer evening starter.

I'm aware that avocados have a negative impact on our environment and for this reason I definitely don't consume them like I used to. If you worry about the impact of avocados but still want to enjoy eating them, one tip that I follow is to eat a quarter of the avocado at a time. That means that one avocado can last you four meals instead of just one.

Preheat your oven to 200°C. Put your sweet potatoes and chickpeas on to a baking sheet, add a drizzle of olive oil and seasoning. Bake for 12–15 minutes, or until lightly golden brown around the edges, then remove from the heat and allow to cool to room temperature.

Rinse the lettuce and dry it, then carefully separate each leaf keeping the cup shape intact, if possible.

To make up each lettuce cup, spoon a few pieces of sweet potato and chickpeas into the centre. Next, add your avocado (about 2 slivers), cherry tomatoes and a few slices of your cucumber. Sprinkle the toasted seeds and chopped coriander on top. Add some lime zest and juice and a light drizzle of olive oil. Additionally, you can add that uneaten pear that's been sitting in the fruit bowl.

SERVES 2

MISFIT VEGGIES AND CELERY LEAVES

1 tbsp lemon juice
1 tsp Dijon mustard
1 tsp brown sugar
1 tbsp balsamic vinegar
3 tbsp extra virgin olive oil
1 head of radicchio, chopped
large handful of berries, quartered
1 carrot, grated
30g almonds, toasted (see page 35) and chopped
handful of celery leaves (see my tip below for how to avoid wasting the celery heart)
freshly ground black pepper

According to the United Nations Food and Agriculture Organization, the amount of food we waste globally could feed up to 2 billion people. Those unwanted veggies that are lingering in your fridge right now could create a beautiful no-waste salad.

When writing this recipe I used what I had in my fridge so adjust it to what's in yours. Perhaps there are a few pieces of kale that haven't made it in to a dish yet, or half a cucumber that's left over – whatever you do have that hasn't been eaten, could potentially make its way into a misfit salad. Create less waste and be surprised by how easy it is to make something out of nothing.

In a small bowl, combine the lemon juice, mustard, sugar and balsamic vinegar. Whisk with a hand whisk until uniform in colour. Slowly add the oil and some pepper, whisking to combine.

Place the radicchio and berries to a big mixing bowl and lightly add your balsamic vinaigrette and toss. Next, add your shredded unwanted carrot and lightly toasted almonds. To finish, add your celery leaves.

Sometimes the food that is unwanted or never eaten makes the simplest of dishes.

TIP

If you want an easy way to use up celery that's not quite as fresh as it was, put it into your juicer, if you have one, or chop it and put it into a high-speed blender with some water.

SERVES 4–6

UPCYCLED SOURDOUGH, SAUTÉED MUSHROOMS AND FRESH HERBS

½ loaf of stale sourdough (you could use any bread you have at home)

3 tbsp olive oil

2 garlic cloves, thinly sliced or crushed

heaped handful of mushrooms (of your choice)

1 tbsp chopped herbs (parsley, chives, oregano)

For the zingy tahini dressing

2 tbsp tahini

½ lemon, juiced and zest

1 tbsp extra virgin olive oil

pinch of salt

1 tbsp olive oil

pinch of black pepper

splash of water

To serve (optional)

green salad

Twenty-four million slices of bread. That is the amount of bread that is wasted each day in the UK alone. Looking at this figure breaks my heart because 1) I love bread and 2) wasting bread doesn't need to happen, ever. It is entirely needless. Here is one of my favourite open-faced sandwiches that you can try when your bread is past the fresh sandwich stage.

Preheat your oven to 120°C. Combine all the dressing ingredients in a small mixing bowl. Whisk well for a few minutes until smooth and creamy. It should thicken, change colour slightly and be easy to pour.

Wet a tea towel and wring until damp. Wrap the loaf of bread in the damp cloth and place in the oven for 2–5 minutes, checking periodically to see if it has softened.

Once the bread has softened, cut it into long slices.

Put the oil, sliced garlic and seasoning into a frying pan over a medium heat. Fry for 2 minutes then add your sliced bread. Toast both sides of bread for 2–3 minutes, or until the edges become crispy and brown. You can place a cup or something with weight on the bread to toast it evenly.

Remove the toast and then, reusing the frying pan, add the mushrooms and sauté. If you feel adventurous, drizzle a small amount of the dressing into the frying pan to sauté with the mushrooms.

To serve, assemble your crispy garlic bread, layering mushrooms and freshly chopped herbs. Drizzle dressing over the top and enjoy. Served well with a side salad or a soup on a cold and chilly evening.

TIP

Did you know that you can bring life back to a stale loaf of bread? Wrap it in a damp tea towel, place in a warm oven for a few minutes and voilà! If I know I won't get through a loaf during the week, I slice it up and freeze it for future use.

MAKES 450G

TOMATO AND CRISPY SAGE HUMMUS

Do you remember your first time? And by that I mean your first time trying hummus, of course. I think the world stopped for a moment when I first tried this food of the gods. My best friend Leo loves hummus and when I say loves hummus, he barrels through it like it's his job. It was him who offered me my first carrot stick and hummus and my taste buds went through the equivalent of the Spanish inquisition. 'Why have you been hiding this from me my whole life?', they yelled.

2 x 400g cans chickpeas (or any white bean or kidney bean), drained and rinsed (see tip below)
2 tbsp lemon juice
2 tbsp tahini
3 sun-dried tomatoes
½ tsp salt
½ tsp ground cumin
½ tsp smoked paprika

For the crispy sage

1 tbsp olive oil
2 garlic cloves, sliced
3 tbsp chopped fresh sage

To serve

pita bread or crudités

Put the chickpeas into a food processor with all the remaining hummus ingredients and purée until creamy and smooth.

To make the crispy sage, heat the oil in a small frying pan over a medium heat. Add the garlic and sage and sauté for a few minutes until it starts to brown slightly.

Put your hummus into a bowl and gently stir through the crispy sage and its oil.

Serve immediately with pita or crudités of your choice. Or spread on some toast or bread for a sandwich. Store in the fridge up to 5 days, but I'm sure it will be eaten before then.

TIP

Make sure you save the water from the chickpea cans and use it to make Aquafaba butter, see page 178, and my Chocolate-dipped coconut macaroons, see page 130.

SERVES 4–6 AS A STARTER, 2 AS A MAIN

CRISPY POTATO BRUSCHETTA

Give me a crispy potato any day of the week. There is something so satisfying about munching into a thin crispy potato so I thought it would make a great swap for the traditional bread for a change. Have you ever had a meal that you thought – wow, everyone needs to know about this? This is a bangin' starter shared with friends or a main for two. It can be served directly on the baking tray to keep those potatoes warm at the start of every bite. Plus, there's less to wash up.

2 large potatoes, unpeeled cut into 5mm-thick rounds
2 tsp olive oil
pinch paprika
350g cherry tomatoes
2 garlic cloves, chopped
small handful of basil (wilted is fine), chopped
1 tbsp fresh lemon juice
1 tbsp balsamic vinegar
1 large ripe avocado, diced
salt and pepper

Preheat your oven to 220°C. Toss your sliced potatoes in a bowl with the olive oil.

Lift your potatoes out the oil on to a baking tray (allowing any excess oil to drip back into the bowl – save this) and season them with a pinch of salt, black pepper and paprika. Spread them evenly into rows and bake for 25–30 minutes. Halfway through the baking, flip them over to colour evenly.

In the meantime, prepare your toppings. Place your tomato, garlic and basil in a food processor and pulse only 10–12 times so that they are roughly chopped. Empty and place into the bowl of leftover oil. Add your lemon and balsamic vinegar and stir. Add your diced avocado and a pinch of salt, to taste.

Keeping the potatoes on the baking tray, add about a teaspoon of the avocado and tomato mixture to each crisp. Finish with any leftover basil stems as a garnish.

HOW TO REDUCE YOUR FOOD WASTE IN 7 DAYS

Food waste is a bigger problem than people realise. One quarter of the food thrown away in the US, UK and Europe could feed the world's nearly 1 billion people. It makes you think, doesn't it?

Tossing edible food in the bin doesn't just waste money – it wastes water, transportation, labour, energy, packaging and resources. Discarded food is sent to landfill, where it rots and produces methane gas – the second most common greenhouse gas. In other words, throwing out your food contributes to climate change.

Sadly, it is not an exaggeration to say that food waste is one of the biggest problems facing mankind today. So let's rethink how we buy food; how we store food; how we eat; and how we put food back into the earth.

Here's my challenge for you: a 7-day no-food-waste challenge.

DAY 1: SHOP SMART

Many people tend to buy more than they need when they go food shopping. Before you hit the shops, make a point of using up all of the food that you purchased during your last shopping trip. For anything missing or that needs replenishing, make a list to take with you to the store and only buy what's on that list.

PLEASE PULL
HANDLE
SLOWLY
LIVE PLASTIC FREE
PLASTIC IS POISON
PLASTIC IS PERMANENT
REFUSE PLASTIC

DAY 2: STORE FOOD PROPERLY

Improper storage is one of the major causes of food waste. Many people are unsure of how to properly store fruit and vegetables, which can lead to premature ripening and, eventually, rotten produce. For instance, potatoes, tomatoes, garlic, cucumbers and onions are best kept at room temperature and therefore shouldn't be refrigerated. The stems of leafy greens and herbs can be submerged in water to keep them fresher for longer. You can store bread in your freezer if you think you won't finish the loaf in time.

DAY 3: SAVE LEFTOVERS (AND ACTUALLY EAT THEM TOO)

Leftovers aren't just for the holidays. If you happen to cook a lot and you regularly have leftovers, designate a day of the week to use up any that have accumulated in the fridge. It's a great way to avoid throwing away food and also saves you time and money. Try to eat and cook fruit and veggies whole without neglecting a single morsel – if it's edible, get the most value out of it as possible.

CHALLENGE YOURSELF TO SEE LEFTOVER FOOD AS A NEW OPPORTUNITY, HARNESS THE 360 DEGREE VIEW!

DAY 4: MAKE A HOMEMADE STOCK

Whipping up a homemade stock is an easy way to reduce food waste. See my recipe on page 176.

DAY 5: MAKE FRIENDS WITH YOUR FREEZER

Freezing food is one of the easiest ways to preserve it, and the types of food that freeze well are endless. For example, greens that are a bit too soft to be used in your favourite salad can be put in freezer bags or containers and used at a later date in smoothies. An excess of herbs can be combined with olive oil and chopped garlic and then frozen in ice-cube trays for a handy and delicious addition to stir fries and other dishes.

You can freeze leftovers from meals; excess produce from your farmers' market haul; and dishes like soups and stews. It's a great way to ensure you always have a healthy, home-cooked meal available.

DAY 6: PACK YOUR LUNCH

A helpful way to save money while reducing your carbon footprint is to bring your lunch to work with you. If you're strapped for time in the morning, try freezing your leftovers or batch cooking in portion-sized containers. That way, you'll have pre-made lunches ready to go each morning.

DAY 7: COMPOST IF YOU CAN

Composting leftover food is a beneficial way to reuse food scraps, turning food waste into energy for plants. While not everyone has a garden with room for an outdoor compost pile (especially if you live in the city), there are lots of countertop composting systems that make this practice easy and accessible for everyone, even those with limited space. Turn to page 58 for my guide to composting.

SERVES 4–6

ZERO-WASTE KALE STEM PESTO WITH GREENS

Sometimes I just need to refuel and nourish myself with (all these) greens. I have a couple of different approaches to making salads – the loud and colourful or the zen minimalist approach like this one. Either way, both are packed with nutrients and flavour to give your taste buds something to talk about.

large bunch of kale, leaves removed and thinly sliced (stems to be used in the pesto)

½ medium green cabbage, cored and thinly sliced (you want long strands of cabbage)

2 small endives, cores removed (compost or save for veggie stock) and thinly sliced

grated zest of ½ lemon

For the pesto

80g kale stems, finely chopped

1 garlic clove, thinly sliced

¾ cup nutritional yeast

1 tbsp fresh lemon juice

60ml water from the steamed kale

35g walnuts

40ml extra virgin olive oil

salt

To serve (optional)

hemp seeds

toasted pumpkin seeds

To make the pesto, add your kale stems to a small saucepan of boiling water and allow to soften. Once the stems are soft, remove with a spoon and place them in a small high-speed blender. Add the garlic, nutritional yeast, lemon juice, kale water, a pinch of salt and the walnuts. Give this a good blend and slowly start to add your oil, until the pesto is to your desired consistency. Want it to be chunkier? Add more walnuts, or if you want it to be smoother – add more kale water.

Place the kale leaves in a big salad bowl, add the cabbage and endives and one heaped spoonful of pesto – fold and stir well. Continue to add one spoonful at a time until the greens are nicely coated.

Top with hemp seeds, toasted pumpkin seeds or avocado slices. Finish by sprinkling over the lemon zest.

L♥VE

MAKES 16

ALL ON YOUR OWN TORTILLAS

The majority of shop-bought tortillas are packaged in plastic and have been sitting on the shelf for weeks, maybe even months. Why not cook your own from scratch? Like anything worthwhile, the recipe takes a little effort, but don't worry, it is quick. You'll never need to buy shop-bought, plastic-packaged tortillas again amigos!

- 480g plain flour, plus extra for dusting
- 1 tsp salt
- 1 tsp baking powder
- 180ml warm water
- 50ml extra virgin olive oil or avocado oil

Filling ideas

- sautéed mushrooms
- avocado, sliced
- corn salsa
- pickled red onions
- coriander

Combine the flour, salt and baking powder in a bowl and mix well. Slowly add your water and oil to the bowl and mix until everything is evenly combined. Transfer your dough to a lightly floured work surface and divide into 16 equal portions. Coat each portion with flour and form into a ball. Flatten with the palm of your hand and cover the pieces with kitchen paper for 15–20 minutes before proceeding.

Begin to roll the dough into rough circles – do your best to keep them 12–15cm in diameter and be sure to keep the work surface and rolling pin lightly floured. Don't stack uncooked tortillas or they will stick together.

Heat a large frying pan over a medium heat. Once the frying pan is hot, gently place a dough circle into it and allow to cook for 30 seconds to 1 minute, or until the underneath has a few pale brown spots and the uncooked surface forms a few bubbles. If browning too quickly, reduce the heat to low. Flip on to the other side and cook for 20–25 seconds. The tortillas should be soft, but have a few small brown spots on the surface. Once finished, keep the tortillas wrapped in or covered with a tea towel

You can have anything with these tortillas and eat them whenever you want – breakfast, lunch, dinner or even as pudding – ice cream tacos!

Add some sautéed mushrooms, slices of avocado, corn salsa, pickled red onions and freshly chopped coriander. Or they're perfect served with the Spicy cauliflower walnut meat overleaf.

TIP

Wrap any leftover tortillas in a tea towel and store in a cupboard or bread tin for up to 7 days. If they start to harden, revive them by sprinkling them with a little water and heat in a frying pan on a low heat.

MAKES ENOUGH TO FILL 6–8 TORTILLAS

SPICY CAULIFLOWER WALNUT MEAT

Nowadays, it's easy to walk into a supermarket and pick out an assortment of substitute meats, but they're always wrapped in plastic so to keep a no-waste lifestyle going we have to get creative. One day perhaps we will have a package-free aisle for all products in every food shop and supermarket around the world but until then we have to make our own substitutes. Not only is this recipe delicious, it's completely plastic-free, so our oceans and earth will thank you. It goes well with basically anything (apart from dessert).

1 head of cauliflower, florets, core and leaves chopped
250g walnuts
2 tsp lime juice (optional)
1 tsp ground cumin
1 tbsp chili powder
1 tbsp extra virgin olive oil

To serve (optional)

All on your own tortillas (see page 80)
pickled red onions (see page 90)
charred asparagus
refried beans
coriander

Begin by preheating your oven to 190°C.

Pulse the cauliflower, walnuts and lime juice in a food processor until they are roughly combined. Then add in your spices, oil and pulse again.

Transfer to a lightly greased baking tray (no parchment paper is needed) and bake for 20–25 minutes. You will want to stir halfway through to have an even bake.

Serve in tortillas with pickled red onions, charred asparagus, refried beans and freshly chopped coriander – or whatever you fancy.

TIP

Store leftovers in an airtight container in the fridge for up to 2 days.

MAKES 6–8

EMPTY-YOUR-FRIDGE ROLL UPS

1 large carrot, cut into matchsticks

1 large cucumber, cut into matchsticks

200g rice or quinoa, cooked

1 pepper (any colour), cut into thin strips

handful of spinach, chopped (or kale)

handful of cooked kidney beans, or any bean will do

6-8 spring greens, leaves only (keep the stems for making veggie stock)

For the roasted beetroot hummus

1 beetroot, cut in quarters

100g dried chickpeas (see page 160 for how to cook yours from scratch) or about 220g canned

1 garlic clove, thinly sliced

1 heaped spoonful tahini

salt and pepepr to taste

pinch of paprika

2 tbsp extra virgin olive oil

chopped coriander (if you have any that needs using up)

This has always been a favourite of mine because you can put anything into these rolls and they will taste phenomenal. Making this dish is never pre-planned and little effort is required. It is for when you have food that may be going to waste soon, but you don't want to chuck it in the bin. As long as you have cabbage or collard greens and a variety of vegetables, you're good to go! This is a great opportunity to get creative . . .

Start by placing your beetroot for the hummus in a large saucepan of boiling water and allow it to simmer for 20–25 minutes, until soft and tender. Drain and leave to cool.

Place all the hummus ingredients except the olive oil and coriander in a food processor and begin to blend on a low speed. After 1 minute, slowly add your olive oil and continue processing until smooth. Transfer the hummus to a bowl for serving and sprinkle your chopped coriander on top. You can either use the hummus as a dip for the rolls or to line the green rolls before filling them.

For the rolls, arrange your fillings on the spring green leaves (spreading them with hummus first if you're going down that route). Fold the ends in and roll from front to back, trying to keep everything nice and cosy.

TIP

You can soften the spring greens leaves by steaming them, reusing the water you used to cook the beetroot. Or keep the beetroot water to make tortillas (see page 80), stored in an airtight container in the freezer with about 7cm of space above the liquid to allow it to expand during the freezing process. Or use it to water your plants or trees outdoors.

SERVES 4, AS A STARTER

WATERMELON, CUCUMBER AND AVOCADO

When summer comes around I love nourishing my body with cooling and refreshing foods, such as watermelon. Watermelon was my favourite fruit as a child because my mother and I grew them each year in our garden. Now, my first stop is the farmers' market (canvas bag in hand) and if there's watermelon on the stalls that's a win.

Nothing beats simple natural foods. Take this simple salad for example. I know us vegans may get a bad rep for eating rabbit food, but you can't deny the deliciousness of a sweet watermelon and its accompanying mates – cucumber and avocado. It's a great starter on a hot summer afternoon – thank me later.

½ watermelon, cubed (save the other half for a smoothie)

1 large cucumber, thinly sliced

2 avocados (skins can be chopped up for compost and pits saved for dying cloths)

extra virgin olive oil, for dressing

few leaves of fresh basil or mint, chopped

salt

Place your watermelon and cucumber into your serving bowl – you can serve one big salad or create beautiful individual plates. Using a teaspoon, scoop out small dollops of avocado. Add the avocado and drizzle with a light touch of extra virgin olive oil. Sprinkle over the basil or mint and a pinch of salt.

TIP

Want to make it a bit fancy? Add your avocado to a food processor with 1 teaspoon of water and 1 tablespoon of extra virgin olive oil and whizz until smooth and creamy. Add to the base of your plate or drizzle over the salad.

FOUR WAYS TO BECOME A CONSCIOUS CONSUMER

01. LESS IS MORE

Before buying anything make sure you really need it. Ask yourself 'is this necessary in my life or can I live without it?' You might be happier with less.

02. BUY THOUGHTFULLY

There are some purchases we need to make, so think about the life cycle of that product. Think about where it came from and where it may go after you finish using it. Ask yourself, 'can I find it second-hand or produced locally?' and 'where does this go after I'm done using it?'

03. BE CONTENT

'Things' don't define who we are. Want to be rebellious? Be happy with what you already own.

If it doesn't bring you happiness donate/give it to those who may find value in it.

It's easier said than done, but is a good reminder for everything in life. Meditate or practice mindfulness each day for a few minutes. This helps me stay present in the moment and find contentedness.

04. START SMALL

We live in a throwaway society and never really contemplate what happens to something after it leaves us. If you can make one change today that's a step in the right direction and do the best you possibly can.

This makes adjusting your consumption seem manageable and over time you will probably find you want to continue making changes. It's about finding balance and making a few small daily changes – remember no one is perfect – just do your best. You got this!

SERVES 4–5

PEARL BARLEY AND LEMON-ROASTED SHAVED ASPARAGUS

When spring is in full swing that means we're shifting and moving out of our winter cocoons. Get up, Marie Kondo your closet and then make this yummy salad. I'm a lover of hearty green salads and feel amazing after eating them. If you want to keep any leftover salad for lunch the next day, keep the dressing separate; no one likes a soggy salad.

200g pearl barley

400ml homemade vegetable stock (see page 176) or water

200g fresh or canned peas (upcycle that can, see page 200)

2 bunches of asparagus

3 small radishes, thinly sliced

handful of pea shoots (or microgreens, if possible)

10g mint leaves, chopped or torn

35g walnuts, chopped

For the pickled red onion

¼ red onion, thinly sliced

white vinegar

For the dressing

1 tbsp maple syrup (or agave syrup or coconut sugar)

1 tsp home-made mustard (see page 190)

grated zest and juice of 1 lemon (keep the pulp aside)

½ tsp salt

½ tsp ground black pepper

80ml extra virgin olive oil

Begin by pickling the onion. Put the red onion into a small bowl with enough white vinegar just to cover it – it's a quick pickle.

Place all the ingredients for the dressing in a blender, and blend on a high speed until smooth and emulsified. Set aside and keep in the fridge to cool. Keep the leftover citrus pulp to the side for the asparagus.

Place the pearl barley in a sieve and rinse with running water to remove all the starch. Put the rinsed barley and stock (or water) in a small saucepan and place over a high heat. Bring to the boil then reduce the heat, cover and simmer until the liquid is completely absorbed and the pearl barley is soft but chewy, 45–50 minutes. Check the pearl barley halfway through to see if you need to add any liquid.

Preheat your oven to 200°C.

Drain the water from the can of green peas but keep it – the reserved water can be made into my aquafaba butter (see page 178) or added to a homemade stock. Rinse the peas, dry and keep to the side for later.

Using a vegetable peeler, shave the length of the asparagus into long thin strips; for smaller strips, start in the centre of the stalk and peel completely. Repeat until each stalk is shaved and then coarsely chop the tops into bite-sized pieces and set aside.

Place the strips of asparagus in a mixing bowl with the leftover citrus pulp – add a light drizzle of oil and some seasoning and toss everything together. The remnants of the citrus will come into contact with the asparagus and give it a lovely flavour.

Transfer the asparagus and leftover lemon a baking sheet (no parchment is needed #ZeroWaste), and roast for 10 minutes until lightly crispy around the edges. Remove from the oven and set aside to cool.

Lift the pickled red onions out of the vinegar but keep the vinegar to pickle the remaining three quarters of the onion. Store it in a sealed container in your fridge for up to 5 days.

Put your warm pearl barley, peas, roasted asparagus, radishes, peas shoots, mint and walnuts into a large bowl and give it all a good toss. Pour in a large spoonful of dressing and mix, then toss in your pickled red onion to finish and serve. The leftover dressing can be stored a in sealed container for up to 2 weeks in the fridge.

SERVES 4

SUMMER SIMPLICITY SALAD

6 tomatoes, sliced
3 peaches, sliced
1 large cucumber, chopped or diced
1 tbsp extra virgin olive oil
1 tsp balsamic vinegar
1 tbsp fresh basil, chopped or torn
lemon juice and grated zest (optional)
1 tbsp hemp seeds or crushed nuts

When I started cooking, I thought I needed to make elaborate dishes that took hours to prepare; this is simply not the case. In fact, simplicity, in my opinion, is the key to delicious food. And did I mention less waste? This salad is the embodiment of the joyfulness of summer – that time of the year when the farmers' markets and greengrocers are bursting with summer's vibrancy.

Put the tomatoes, peaches and cucumber into a big serving bowl and mix lightly. Drizzle over the olive oil and balsamic vinegar and toss in the basil. Squeeze a little bit of lemon juice or zest over the salad if you fancy and scatter over the seeds or nuts.

03

LESS WASTE DINNER

SERVES 2–4

BROCCOLI STALK SOUP

One evening when I was a kid, my father told me to eat all my broccoli and I refused. He said that if I didn't finish it that I wasn't going to be allowed to leave the table, so I ended up sleeping at the table that night. The next morning I had to get ready for school, but my father pulled me back into the kitchen, reheated my broccoli and waited until I had finished it. Maybe this was the moment I realised that food is important and should never be wasted. Thanks Dad.

We tend only to eat the florets when we cook broccoli, but there's so much goodness and flavour in the stalk. This simple, delicious soup ensures you don't waste anything.

3 large broccoli heads, with stalks and florets separated

1 small leek, chopped

1 litre homemade vegetable stock (see page 176)

extra virgin olive oil

pinch of smoked paprika

large handful of leafy greens (rocket, spinach or kale), plus extra to garnish

1 tsp grated ginger

200ml milk (I prefer coconut for the creaminess)

3 radishes, thinly sliced

salt and pepper

To serve (optional)

handful of cooked leftover peas

Cut the broccoli stalk and florets into 5cm pieces. Bring a saucepan of water to the boil then drop in your broccoli stems, florets and leek. Allow them to simmer for 3–5 minutes. Remove the broccoli and leek from the water – but keep the water to make vegetable stock (see page 176) – see my tip opposite. Set aside a few of the tiny florets from the top of the crown to use as a garnish.

In a separate saucepan, heat your home made stock over a medium–low heat for 5 minutes or to a light simmer.

Add your broccoli and leek to a blender with a hearty splash of extra virgin olive oil, some salt and pepper and the paprika. Next, add the hot vegetable stock, leafy greens and ginger. Blend on a high speed for 2–3 minutes, until smooth and creamy. Slowly add the milk on a low speed.

Serve in a bowl topped with the radishes, reserved broccoli florets and leftover leafy greens. Leftover peas make a great addition, or even some leftover bread made into croutons for a wicked crunch.

TIP

If you don't have enough ingredients to start a stock you can save any water you use to cook vegetables in an airtight, sealed container for up to 5 days.

SERVES 4–8, AS A STARTER

LEFTOVER VEGGIE NACHOS

1 x 200g bag tortilla chips

½ bunch kale, chopped

2 tomatoes, diced

100g dried cannellini beans (or any bean is fine), soaked overnight then cooked (see page 160)

1 large carrot, shaved into ribbons or thinly sliced

olive oil, for drizzling

120ml Cheese sauce (see page 179)

3 tbsp home-made cashew yoghurt (see page 38) or any other yoghurt you like

Pickled red onion (see page 90) or any other pickles you have at home

1 raw beetroot, very finely sliced

small bunch of coriander, chopped

Something I love doing (when invited) is to rummage through my friends' and family's kitchens and see what they have that hasn't been eaten, or worse, has been forgotten.

In a recent visit to a friend's kitchen, I stumbled upon a bag of nachos that had definitely been there at my last visit. I suspected they weren't going to be eaten so I devised this recipe to make use of them. Plus, I haven't bought a bag of nachos or anything in plastic for that matter in almost two years so it was a treat. I know that this plastic-free living may be challenging for some so this recipe is not to encourage you to go out and buy bags of nachos; it was my ticket to preparing a fun and tasty meal from something that was in plastic. But perhaps you love nachos and tortilla chips are the only plastic product you buy. (We made sure to recycle the bag afterwards, of course.)

Preheat your oven to 180°C.

Place the bag of nachos on a baking tray, then cover them with a layer of chopped kale first, then a layer of chopped or crushed tomato and beans.

Add the carrot and a light drizzle of olive oil. Bake in the oven for 8–10 minutes until the edges of the tortilla chips start to brown.

Remove from the oven, but keep everything on the tray. Drizzle over your cheese sauce, a dollop of cashew yoghurt, pickled vegetables, beetroot and coriander.

The best is that it can be eaten straight from the tray and means you'll have less to clean up – that was easy!

SERVES 4–6

WASTE-NOT VEGETABLE STEW

Sometimes we are left with half-used, unwanted ingredients that sit in the fridge for days before being sent to the bin. This stew is an easy way to use up those forgotten ingredients – whether they be wilted or bruised. It's ideal for cooking in a big batch and freezing portions to have for those days when you don't know what to cook, or to have for your lunch the next day.

Note that the focus here is to cook what you already have in your fridge, so nothing goes to waste. If you don't have an aubergine, swap it for a courgette or a yellow squash, and sub the kale for spinach or another leafy green.

2 tbsp olive oil
1 onion, finely chopped
3 garlic cloves, minced
1 aubergine, chopped
500g tomatoes, diced or crushed
350g dried cannellini beans, soaked overnight then cooked (see page 160 for how to cook them)
2 tsp paprika
1 tsp ground cumin
1 tsp dried oregano
pinch of dried chill flakes (optional)
120ml home-made vegetable stock (see page 176)
bunch of kale, chopped
salt and pepper

To serve

small bunch of parsley (stems and leaves), chopped
leftover bread, toasted

Warm the olive oil in a large frying pan over a medium heat, add the onion and fry until translucent, then add your garlic and cook until fragrant.

Now add the aubergine, tomatoes, beans, paprika, cumin, oregano and some salt and pepper – you can even spice it up a bit with some chilli flakes. Stir and combine until it starts to simmer. Simmer for 2 minutes, then add the stock, reduce the heat to a very slow simmer, cover with a lid and cook for 10 minutes. Add the kale and cook for 5 minutes, or until wilted. Check that the aubergine is soft, then remove the pan from the heat, sprinkle over the chopped parsley and serve with toasted leftover bread to soak up the juices.

SERVES 6

PLANTS ONLY SHEPHERD'S PIE

We all have fond memories of the food we ate during our childhood and this dish is particularly dear to my heart. My mother wasn't the chef of the household, but when she did cook everything was sensational and a shepherd's pie is something she loved making on weekends, especially on cold wintery days. I've taken her recipe and have added my twist – packing it with plants in place of the meat, and using all the tops and ends of my vegetables so that nothing goes to waste. If you want to keep this dish vegan be sure to check the back of the wine bottle to make sure it's vegan-friendly or substitute it for balsamic vinegar.

- 6 large seasonal potatoes, peeled and quartered (see opposite for how to make crisps from the peel)
- 1 tbsp olive oil (or aquafaba butter, see page 178)
- 3 carrots, chopped and unpeeled (remove any green tops and chop finely to use as a garnish)
- 400g mushrooms, chopped
- 2 shallots, thinly sliced (save the skins for stock, see page 176)
- 250g fresh garden peas, (or canned, remember to save the can for upcycling, see page 200)
- 1 garlic clove, thinly sliced (save the skin for stock, see page 176)
- 200ml home-made vegetable stock (see page 176)
- 2 tbsp herbs (I like to use half rosemary, half thyme but use any fresh or dried herbs you have at home), plus any extra you have to garnish
- 2 tbsp homemade tomato purée (see page 184)
- 40ml red wine or balsamic vinegar
- 2 tbsp plain flour
- salt and pepper

Preheat your oven to 200°C.

Bring a large saucepan of water to the boil and drop in the potatoes. Cook the potatoes for about 10–15 minutes until they are soft and can easily be forked. Add the olive oil and some salt and black pepper. Mash with a potato masher, until mainly smooth with some chunks.

Put the carrots, mushrooms, shallots, peas and garlic into a large deep frying pan with 1 tablespoon of water (no oil needed here) and cook over a medium heat, stirring occasionally, for 4–5 minutes, until the vegetables have softened, then add the stock and herbs. Cook for 10 minutes, then add the tomato purée and red wine and bring to a light simmer. Over a medium–low heat, stir in the flour and cook until the mixture thickens then transfer it to a heatproof baking dish, about 20 x 25cm.

Spread your mashed potatoes evenly over your vegetables in a thick layer – if you like, drizzle a touch of extra virgin olive oil to the top. Bake for 20 minutes, or until the potatoes begin to brown. Garnish with any reserved carrot tops, extra herbs or crispy potato skins (see opposite) before serving.

TIP

To crisp potato skins, bring a frying pan to a high heat with 2 tablespoons of vegetable oil and drop your potato skins in for a quick flash fry. After 1–2 minutes, remove from the oil and allow them to drain and dry in a sieve set over a bowl. I reuse the saved oil for roasting veggies by storing it in a small airtighht container.

SERVES 5–6

MEAT-FREE BOLOGNESE

Just because something is meat-free, it doesn't mean it can't have the robust and dense flavour that is typically associated with meat. There's nothing plants can't emulate and this recipe may mean you'll want to commit to a meatless meal on more days than just a Monday.

- 1 tbsp olive oil
- 1 carrot, finely diced
- 1 celery stick, finely diced
- 1 onion, thinly sliced
- 250g chestnut mushrooms, chopped and diced
- ¼ tsp chilli flakes
- 2 tsp dried oregano
- 2 garlic cloves, finely chopped
- 250ml red wine
- 2 tbsp soy sauce (or tamari)
- 2 tbsp tomato purée (see page 184 for how to make your own)
- 5 tomatoes, chopped (or 1 x 400g can, to upcycle the can see page 200)
- 2 bay leaves
- 500ml home made vegetable stock (see page 176) or water
- 85g walnuts, roughly chopped
- 500g spaghetti
- small handfull of basil, chopped or torn
- salt and pepper

Heat a large saucepan over a medium heat and add the oil. Add the carrot, celery and onion and cook until translucent and soft. Add the mushrooms, chilli flakes and oregano and sauté for another 5–7 minutes until soft, then add the garlic.

Add the red wine and soy sauce and bring to the boil then reduce the heat to a simmer. Cook for 10 minutes, stirring occasionally.

Toss in your tomato purée and tomatoes and stir well, then add the bay leaves and stock. Cook for 25–30 minutes at a light simmer until the liquid has reduced and the sauce has thickened.

Next, add your walnuts to the sauce for another 5 minutes, stirring well. Add a pinch of salt and pepper now and stir.

Meanwhile, cook the spaghetti to your liking, then drain.

To serve, divide you spaghetti between the bowls, add a spoonful of mushroom-walnut bolognese, sprinkle the basil over each bowl and enjoy. Buon appetito!

TIP

Store leftovers in the fridge for 3 days or in the freezer for up to 1 month.

SERVES 4–5

SEED TO SKIN SQUASH AND SAGE PASTA

As we transition to autumn and its colder and darker days, all I crave is a warm bowl of hearty deliciousness. One vegetable I never ate when I was growing up was butternut squash – I think my parents thought we wouldn't like it. Well, they hadn't tried adding it to pasta! In this dish the skins can be peeled then roasted or simply left on. Save the seeds as you can toast them and have them as a snack or use them to add extra crunch to a soup or salad.

5–7 sage leaves (or 1 tbsp dried sage)

1 butternut squash, peeled, deseeded and chopped (keep the skin and seeds)

extra virgin olive oil

2 garlic cloves, peeled (save the skins for your vegetable stock or compost them)

1 onion, quartered

1 tsp paprika

200ml milk (I like coconut but use any you have)

500g pasta (I like pappardelle for its thickness and because the lengths pick up more of the sauce)

salt and pepper

To serve

handful of rocket or shredded kale

Preheat your oven to 200°C.

In a bowl, mix the sage, squash seeds and skins with a tablespoon of olive oil and some salt and pepper. Place on a baking tray and roast in the oven for 15–20 minutes. Remove from the tray once roasted and lightly crisped. Separate the sage, seeds and skins for later.

Put your butternut squash, garlic and onion on the same baking tray with a light drizzle of olive oil and a sprinkle of salt, pepper and the paprika. Roast in the oven for 40–45 minutes, until the edges begin to brown and crisp and the flesh is soft.

Once ready, leave to cool on the baking tray.

To a blender or food processor, add your roasted garlic and onion and half of the milk. Give this a good blend until smooth and creamy. Add the roasted butternut squash, a few leaves of roasted sage and a pinch of salt and pepper. Pulse until thick and a bit chunky still – if you blend at a high speed continuously you'll end up making a soup.

Cook the pasta until tender (or cooked to your liking), then transfer to a serving bowl with heaping spoonfuls of the sauce and toss to coat evenly. Serve with the roasted pumpkin skins and toasted seeds. Adding a bit of leafy greens like rocket or shredded kale can really give this dish more nutritional value (we musn't forget our greens).

SERVES 4–6, WITH LEFTOVERS

CAULIFLOWER CURRY WITH GINGER JASMINE RICE

For this dish, I want you to have leftovers so you can discover just how incredibly delicious they can be. Thank me later!

2 tbsp coconut oil
½ tsp mustard seeds
½ tsp fennel seeds
½ tsp coriander seeds
½ tsp black pepper
1 tsp turmeric (freshly grated or ground)
½ tsp cumin
pinch of cayenne pepper
pinch of ground cinnamon
grated zest of ½ orange
2 garlic cloves, grated
1 yellow onion, diced
1½ carrot, chopped
1–2 tbsp ginger, grated
1 large cauliflower, florets, core and leaves
500ml homemade vegetable stock (see page 176)
4–5 plum tomatoes, quartered
35ml canned coconut milk (upcycle the can, see page 200)

For the ginger jasmine rice

1 tbsp coconut oil
1 garlic clove, grated or minced
1 tbsp grated ginger
pinch of salt
200g jasmine rice, rinsed
½ carrot, grated (use the other half for the curry)

To serve

small bunch of coriander, chopped
homemade cashew yoghurt (see page 38)

Start by making the rice. Put a medium saucepan over a medium heat, then add your coconut oil and leave it to melt. Add the garlic, ginger and salt and give that a good stir to coat everything nicely. After 2 minutes, or when the garlic and ginger begin to crisp, add your rice and stir well.

After about 1–2 minutes, add 240ml of water. Bring to the boil, cover the saucepan with a lid and reduce your heat to low. Leave your rice alone for the next 10–15 minutes to cook – it should be light and fluffy. Lightly dry your grated carrot with a cloth and stir it into the rice for the last 3 minutes of cooking. Remove from the heat and set aside until you're ready to serve.

For the curry, put a large saucepan over a medium–high heat and add the coconut oil. Once melted, throw in all your spices and orange zest and give that a good stir, coating all the spices with the oil. Add the garlic, onion, carrot and ginger and cook for 5 minutes, stirring frequently. Cut or tear apart the cauliflower with your hands into bite-sized pieces, then add it to the pan, with the stock (or water). Bring to the boil and add the tomatoes. Reduce the heat to low, cover with a lid and allow to cook for on the lowest heat for 30 minutes. Remove from the heat and allow to sit for 15 minutes before serving.

Remove the pan from the heat, add the coconut milk and give the curry a good stir. Serve in bowls topped with chopped coriander, toasted pumpkin seeds and a yummy dollop of homemade cashew yoghurt.

FOOD THAT MAGICALLY REGROWS ITSELF

Growing anything from seed is impressive, but also difficult, unless you've been blessed with green fingers. Sure it saves on money, but there has to be an easier way, and there is! You can actually grow food from your very own kitchen scraps. There is something pretty amazing about regrowing your food – more food, less waste, saves money. You can upcycle everything from celery scraps to onion roots with a great chance of success. Transform your food scraps!

SPRING ONIONS, LEEKS, FENNEL, LEMONGRASS, CORIANDER, BASIL AND MINT

» Place the root ends in a glass of water but don't submerge them fully.

» Change the water daily.

» In 2–5 days, growth should begin.

» Harvest the greens when full by simply cutting off what you need without uprooting the plant. You can keep it submerged in water for a one-off, but if you want to continue to have sustainable growth, place in a pot of soil and grow all year round.

CELERY, CABBAGE, ROMAINE LETTUCE AND BOK CHOY

» Submerge the roots in a deep bowl, leaving the tops above the water line.

» Spray with water a couple of times a week, replacing the water every few days.

» Leaves will sprout in about a week.

» Plant the cutting in a pot indoors or in a garden with only the leaves above the soil.

» Harvest when fully grown, after about 5 months.

GINGER

» Soak a 2.5–5cm chunk of ginger in water overnight.

» The next day, place the ginger root in soil with the eye bud pointing up and cover it with 2.5–5cm more soil. Water lightly.

» Place the pot in a spot that stays warm but doesn't get a lot of bright light. Keep the soil moist, being careful not to over-water it.

» Ginger is slow to grow so be patient. After 2–3 weeks you should see some shoots appear: simply remove the entire plant, use what you need and repeat.

ONION

» Place the root end in a small pot of soil and lightly cover it in soil.

» Keep thhe soil moist.

» You will start to see budding onions in about a week. Carefully separate the new onions, leaving the roots attached, and plant them in a larger pot, or in your garden. Occasionally, cut the leaves down to promote full growth.

» It can take up to 5 months for plants to mature enough for you to harvest them.

GARLIC

- Once your garlic has sprouted a green shoot, plant the whole bulb in the ground or in a pot of soil leaving only the shoot to appear. The larger the clove, the larger the resulting bulb.
- Sit the plant in a sunny window, keeping the soil moist.
- The bulbs will be ready for harvest when the bottom third of the leaves has yellowed.

MUSHROOMS

- Put about 5cm of compost or used coffee grounds in a sterile large Mason jar.
- Add 2-3 mushroom stalks/caps to the top of the compost with only their surface exposed and cover with a tea towel.
- If the cutting takes, new growth happens quickly (within 48 hours).
- Harvest and repeat.

PINEAPPLE

- Don't live in the tropics? That's okay, you can bring them to you. You just cut the leafy top off the pineapple. Remove some of the lower leaves to expose the stem. Insert a few toothpicks in the sides of the stem at a 90° angle to it, then suspend the pineapple over a large jar of water, with the base of the stem sitting in the water (the toothpicks will hold it in place).
- Keep the container in direct sunlight. If it is warm outside, sit it on the porch or deck during the day and bring it in at night.
- Change the water every other day or so. You will then notice roots in about a week or two and once they are formed you can transfer the pineapple crown into potting soil. If you live in a cooler area, (i.e. not the tropics) it is best to grow your pineapple in a container indoors.

SERVES 4–5

CRISPY ORANGE AUBERGINE AND GINGER GARLIC BROCCOLI

For the first 20 years of my life, I didn't know what an aubergine was. But when I moved away to New York City, I saw them in every supermarket and I had to find out what they were and how I could eat them. It is a vegetable I've grown to like a lot and use in more and more of my cooking because of its versatility. You can bake an aubergine, have it in a curry or stew, turn it into a dip. It's now a star vegetable in my kitchen.

grated zest and juice of 2 oranges (see pages 125 and 202–3 for how to use your citrus waste)

olive oil

80g leftover bread (or breadcrumbs)

2 large aubergines, cut into 2.5cm cubes (use the stem for stock or compost)

2 large crowns of broccoli, broken into florets (save the stalks for the Broccoli Soup on page 97)

1 tsp sesame oil

thumb-sized piece of ginger, thinly sliced

1 garlic clove, thinly sliced

To serve

brown rice or cauliflower rice (see page 166)

sesame seeds

tamari

Preheat your oven to 200°C.

Mix the orange juice with half the zest, a glug of oil and whisk until smooth and creamy-like. Pulse your leftover bread to make fine breadcrumbs and place them in another shallow bowl.

Dry the aubergine cubes with a tea towel to remove excess water. Drop the cubed aubergine into the orange mixture then place them in the breadcrumbs. Transfer all the breaded aubergine to a baking tray (no parchment paper needed). Roast for 15–20 minutes, until lightly brown, checking periodically to ensure nothing burns.

Meanwhile, bring a saucepan of water to the boil and drop in your broccoli. Cook for 3–5 minutes over a medium heat. Once you're able to poke the stems of the broccoli with a fork easily, drain.

Put the sesame oil into a frying pan set over a medium–high heat, then add the ginger and garlic. Fry, stirring occasionally, to allow it to crisp and brown evenly. After about 2 minutes remove from the heat, drain the oil from the pan into a bowl and place the ginger and garlic slices on some kitchen towel to remove any excess oil – this will help dry them so that they become even more crispy.

Put your cooked brown rice or cauliflower rice into bowls. Add the crispy orange aubergine and broccoli and garnish with the crispy ginger and garlic. Spoon the leftover oil over each dish. and sprinkle over a few sesame seeds and some tamari. Garnish with the remaining orange zest.

SERVES 4–6

SWEET POTATO DHAL AND MANGO COCONUT RICE

Fold down the corner of this page now because this one is my absolute favourite. Warm, creamy dhal and sweet fragrant rice is something I would have at least four times per week, but my girlfriend Venetia wants more variety – yes, dear!

I never knew what dhal was until I moved to Los Angeles in 2016 and was living near a yogi community. The delicious and fragrant aromas left my taste buds wanting more and the simplicity of making something so delightful soothes my soul and nourishes my body with every bite. Leftovers, please.

- 2 small sweet potatoes, (or peeled but use the peel to make crisps, see page 103), cut into 1.5 cubes
- ½ tsp fennel seeds
- ½ tsp ground cumin
- olive oil, for roasting
- 1 tbsp coconut oil
- 2 garlic cloves, peeled and crushed
- 1 onion, thinly sliced
- 5cm piece of fresh ginger, chopped
- 1 tsp cumin seeds
- 1 tsp coriander seeds
- 1 tsp ground cinnamon
- 1 tsp turmeric (fresh or ground)
- 1 tsp black mustard seeds
- ½ tsp paprika
- ½ tsp black pepper
- 200g yellow split peas, soaked in cold water for 1 hour (or any lentils of your choice)
- 500ml homemade vegetable stock (see page 176) or water
- 1 x 400ml can coconut milk
- 2 large handfuls of spinach (kale or swiss chard, optional)
- grated zest of 1 lemon
- bunch of coriander, chopped (stalks and all)
- salt and pepper
- homemade naan (see page 182) , to serve

Preheat the oven to 180°C. Place your sweet potato on a baking tray and add the fennel seeds, ground cumin, salt and pepper and a drizzle of olive oil. Roast in the oven at for 20 minutes until soft, sweet and little crispy around the edges.

In a large saucepan, melt the coconut oil then sauté your garlic, onion and ginger over a low heat for a few minutes until soft. Either grind the cumin and coriander seeds in a pestle and mortar or add to the saucepan whole. Next, add the remaining spices to the pan. Stir everything until well coated for 5 minutes and turn the heat up to medium. Add the split peas and vegetable stock to the pan and bring to a light simmer. Reduce the heat and cook for 1 hour.

Add the coconut milk for the last few minutes of cooking and stir well. Remove the pan from the heat and stir in the spinach and lemon zest. Add the sweet potato and half the chopped coriander.

For the rice, put the desiccated coconut into a dry saucepan set over a medium heat. Toast the coconut for a few minutes but be sure not to let it burn. Remove and set aside. Add the rice to the pan with 150ml water and stir for a moment. Bring to a light simmer for 5 minutes, then reduce the heat to low and cover. Check it periodically but don't stir it or your rice will be starchy. Cook for 15 minutes, or until light and fluffy, then remove from the heat and add your desiccated coconut and chopped mango and stir.

Serve the dhal and rice in bowls topped with the rest of your chopped coriander and perhaps some home made naan breads.

For the mango coconut rice

20g desiccated coconut

200g jasmine rice, soaked and rinsed

½ mango, chopped

MAKES 6 PATTIES

STEMS-AND-ALL GREEN BURGER

My ultimate indulgence is burgers, with large portions of fries and a big dollop of ketchup, with a chocolate milkshake on the side – after all, I am American. I don't call burgers 'vegan burgers', they're all just burgers to me now. Today, meat-free burger companies are making huge waves, but I prefer my burgers to be made with nothing but plants, which means I make my own. This burger is loaded with nutrients to leave you feeling satisfied.

- handful of spinach (stems and all)
- handful of rocket
- ½ bunch coriander (stems and all)
- ½ bunch dill
- 1 garlic clove, thinly sliced
- 60g dried chickpeas, soaked for 24 hours then cooked (see page 160) or 1 x 200g can, drained
- 130g dried cannellini beans, soaked for 24 hours then cooked (see page 160) or 1 x 400g can, drained
- 70g peas (fresh or canned – upcycle that can, see page 200)
- 130g chestnut mushrooms
- 100g oat flour (or any flour you have)
- 2 tbsp extra virgin olive oil
- cayenne pepper
- dried parsley
- salt and pepper

For the flax egg

- 1 tbsp ground flax seeds
- 3 tbsp water

To serve

- burger buns
- crisp lettuce
- sliced tomato
- red onion
- homemade cheese sauce (see page 179)
- homemade chips (see page 193)

In a food processor, on a low speed, pulse your spinach, rocket, fresh herbs and garlic for 20 seconds into a paste-like consistency. Next, add your chickpeas, beans, peas, mushrooms, oat flour and extra virgin olive oil and pulse again until you have a rough paste.

Preheat your oven to 200°C.

In a separate small mixing bowl, make your flax egg by mixing the flaxseeds with the water and whisking with a fork for 1 minute. Allow this to sit for 5 minutes to coagulate, then add your flax egg to the paste in the processor and blend. Transfer the mixture to a large bowl and mix in the spices, using your hands and making sure everything is evenly combined.

Using your palms, shape the mixture into 6 small burger patties and place them on a baking sheet (no parchment is needed). Bake in the oven for 15–20 minutes, or until the edges start to crisp and brown.

Serve on a bun, with crisp lettuce, sliced tomato, red onion, cheese and homemade chips (and don't forget the chocolate milkshake!).

SERVES 3–4

'I HAVE NOTHING IN MY FRIDGE' STIR FRY

We've all been there. There are a few odd vegetables hanging around in the fridge, but nothing sparks creativity or inspires you to cook a full meal and you find yourself eating hummus off a spoon. You suddenly feel that you need to go shopping for more food.

My challenge for you is to cook (and eat) everything in your fridge before you shop again. This eliminates food waste, saves a bit of money, and you get to exercise being creative with your meals. All you really need is a few ingredients. I once had a can of chickpeas, one stick of celery and soy sauce – and, yes I made something and it was delicious. You'll have to take my word for that one.

START WITH A GRAIN (CHOOSE 1)

250g quinoa, short-grain brown rice, white rice, jasmine rice or pearl barley

+

ADD A VEGETABLE (CHOOSE 1–2)

broccoli, aubergine, cauliflower, mushroom, peppers, leeks

+

ADD FLAVOUR (CHOOSE AS MANY AS YOU LIKE)

pickled ginger, roasted garlic, roasted red peppers, sautéed onions

+

ADD A RAW LEAFY GREEN (CHOOSE 1)

spinach, shredded kale, Swiss chard, little gem, watercress, cabbage

+

TO SERVE (OPTIONAL)

avocado

1 tbsp toasted seeds

2 tbsp leftover hummus

Begin by steaming your grain. Bring 325ml of water to a light boil, add your grain and stir. Reduce the heat, cover with a lid and cook for 15–20 minutes or until light, fluffy and chewy.

Meanwhile add 1 tablespoon of sesame oil to a frying pan over a medium–high heat. Add your vegetable(s) and cook for 2 minutes. Next, add your flavour(s) and stir frequently to coat all the ingredients.

Chop your green, add it to the pan and cook until wilted.

Serve in a bowl. If you have an avocado, toasted seeds or even that leftover hummus it will go nicely as an addition.

MAKES 2 LARGE PIZZAS OR 8 PIZZETTE

DOUGH BOY PIZZA

Pizza is – and has always been – one of the most important things in my life. My father taught me how to make dough from scratch at a young age, and my first paying job at the age of 16 was working in a pizza restaurant; I was the dough boy. In short, you're getting a 20-year-old recipe.

130g plain flour
130g wholemeal flour
1 tsp salt
180ml warm water
¾ tsp dried active yeast
1 tsp extra virgin olive oil
semolina, for dusting

For the topping(s)

homemade tomato purée or cheese sauce (see pages 184 and 179)

mushrooms, onion, garlic, roasted peppers, extra virgin olive oil

shaved Brussels sprouts, crushed walnuts and sesame seeds

In a large mixing bowl, combine your flours and salt.

In another large mixing bowl, begin to whisk the warm water, yeast and olive oil until it starts to foam a bit, then pour it straight into the flour mixture. Knead the mixture with your hands until everything is combined well, then cover with a tea towel and set aside for 20–30 minutes.

On a floured surface, knead the rested dough for 2 minutes. Cut the dough in half and roll each piece into a ball. You may need to sprinkle a bit of flour so it doesn't stick to your hands. Place the dough in two separate bowls or keep on a flour dusted surfaced covered with a cloth for 3–4 hours.

Preheat the oven to 220°C.

Place each ball of dough separately on a floured surface and begin to stretch the dough using your fingers (if you're making pizzettes, cut the dough from each bowl into four and roll into eight small balls). Press the dough with your hands to flatten it out or use a rolling pin to roll it out to 15-17cm in diameter for pizzettes.

Dust two baking trays with some semolina and place 1 pizza or 4 pizzettes gently on each tray. Add your preferred base and any toppings you like. I usually go for either a light tomato base with mushrooms, onion, garlic and peppers, finished with a light drizzle of olive oil, some pepper and a pinch of salt, or my cheese sauce with some shaved Brussels sprouts, crushed walnuts and sesame seeds.

ZERO-WASTE LIFE HACKS FOR THE HOME

Becoming more sustainable in your everyday life is usually about taking small steps and eventually you'll introduce bigger changes. Sometimes it's just asking yourself 'Why am I throwing this away?' Or 'is there anything I can use this for?' And this goes beyond the stuff you cook at home. Simply challenging the everyday norms, like refusing plastic straws in your drinks, paper napkins, even a cardboard drinks coaster at the pub. Becoming more sustainable in your everyday life is an on-going process.

CITRUS BOMB HOUSE CLEANER

I had no idea that our typical house cleaners were potentially toxic. When I started introducing zero-waste habits and choices into my life I had to look at everything that I purchased and consumed. I had no idea how easy it was to make your own house cleaner from potential food waste. For this cleaner you just need to keep saving your citrus peel in a sealed container in the freezer, until you have a good handful or two (about 5–8 lemons or oranges).

Vinegar makes a great cleaner as it cuts through tough grease, grime and mineral deposits but it's important to remember when NOT to use it, so not on granite, marble, soapstone, kitchen knives or solid wood.

The power of vinegar is great, but I don't want my toilet or sink to always smell like salad dressing so enter citrus and this sweet-smelling house cleaner.

large handful of leftover citrus peel (see above)
white vinegar
essential oil (optional)
old spray bottle

Put your peel into a large sealable container and cover with white vinegar. Seal the lid and leave to infuse for 2–3 weeks. Afterwards, mix equal parts water with the citrus vinegar and transfer it to old spray bottle. Add a few drops of essential oils you like.

THE FRIDGE FRESHENER

At some point in your life, you've come into your kitchen, opened your fridge door looking for something delicious to eat and all of a sudden are smacked in the face with a horrible odour.

What you are experiencing is a smell that is made up of food particles that float around and eventually settle on other foods which isn't exactly what you want to be tasting. Thankfully you can keep your fridge smelling so fresh and so clean with this easy do-it-yourself hack that can keep your fridge odour-free.

100g bicarbonate of soda
small Mason jar
10 drops essential oil
small kitchen cloth

Put the bicarbonate of soda into a small Mason jar and add the essential oil. Place a small cloth over the opening. Place in the back of fridge up to 3 months.

Smelly compost? Dirty bird bath? When your fridge freshener is finished, add it to a compost or use it to wash out your bird bath. #NoWaste

DIY INSECT REPELLENT

I don't trust what's in those single-use plastic insect repellent bottles, so I make my own. You can normally find witch hazel in your pharmacy or online in a glass bottle so stock up on your homemade insect repellent before you travel.

90ml filtered water
½ tsp witch hazel
3 tbsp jojoba oil
20 drops of essential oil (lavender, lemon, peppermint or sandalwood)

Stir or shake all the ingredients in a reusable sealed container. Pour the mixture into a spray bottle and shake well before using.

PLASTIC-FREE LAUNDRY DETERGENT

Time to ditch the plastic bottles on laundry detergent and make yours from scratch. DIY cleaners can be much safer for your family and the environment.

1 large bar of soap (about 190g), grated using the large holes of a box grater
220g bicarbonate of soda
250g borax powder
250g washing soda

Simply mix the soap with the other ingredients. Place in a glass container and store in a cupboard.

This soap works best with warm-to-hot-water washing – use 2 tablespoons per wash.

04

SUSTAINABLE SWEETS

MAKES ABOUT 12

CHOCOLATE-DIPPED COCONUT MACAROONS

The first time I ever made these macaroons was on live television and the producer of the show wanted me to create a no-waste winter holiday recipe. In the moment I decided to find a way to make a simple and delicious treat from food that would otherwise have been wasted. This coconutty and chocolatey goodness is made with aquafaba – that's the liquid left over from soaking chickpeas or the liquid from a can of them. Chickpea liquid is a baker's gold.

- 200g desiccated coconut
- 2 tbsp coconut oil, soft but not melted
- 2 tbsp maple syrup
- 1½ tbsp aquafaba (leftover from any canned bean, see page 178)
- 60ml milk (see page 194 for how to make your own)
- pinch of salt
- ½ tsp vanilla extract
- 1 tbsp cornflour
- 50g dark vegan chocolate

Preheat your oven to 190°C.

Put the coconut into a food processor and pulse for 30–45 seconds, but be careful it doesn't clump or turn into a butter. Add 1 tablespoon of the coconut oil, the maple syrup, aquafaba, milk, salt and vanilla and mix for another 15–20 seconds to combine. Add the cornflour and pulse several times until you have a wet dough.

Scoop out 1–1½ tablespoons of dough (using a measuring spoon) and gently place on a baking tray. They need to have lots of room between them – about 7–10cm (the size of your fist).

Bake for 12–15 minutes, or until the tops begin to brown lightly, then remove from the oven and leave them to cool on the tray.

To melt the chocolate I use what is called the double boiling technique. Place 3–5cm of water in a small saucepan and bring to a simmer.

Place a small heatproof bowl (ceramic or glass) over the saucepan, making sure that the bottom of the bowl is not touching the water. The double boiler provides heat through steam alone. Add your chocolate and the remaining tablespoon of coconut oil and allow them to melt, stirring frequently, until your chocolate mixture is melted and you have a pourable sauce.

Remove the bowl from the saucepan and set the chocolate aside to cool for 5 minutes, but not completely – you still want a pourable and dippable chocolate.

Dip the underside of each macaroon into the bowl of chocolate, allowing any excess to drip off. Place each dipped macaroon on a plate, then place in the fridge to chill for 10–15 minutes. Store in the freezer for up to 1 month.

MAKES 1 LOAF CAKE

VENETIA'S NO WASTE CARROT CAKE

I've never gone out with someone who truly enjoyed cooking and eating as much as me. It can be quite challenging because at every meal we cook, we always want to impress and please the other. Most nights I cook the main and Venetia handles pudding. She first made this when we prepared a friend his 'death-row dinner'. Her version of his requested cake somewhat stole the glory from my starter and main. And that's why it's in this book!

- 220g buckwheat flour (or plain flour)
- 1½ tsp baking powder
- ½ tsp ground cinnamon
- ½ tsp ground nutmeg
- ½ tsp ground ginger
- 1 tsp salt
- 100g apple sauce from a glass jar
- 200ml milk (see page 194 for how to make your own)
- 1 tsp vanilla extract
- 6 tbsp coconut oil, melted, plus extra for greasing
- 8 tbsp maple syrup (golden syrup or agave work too)
- 2 carrots, grated (keep the peel on)
- 50g chopped dates (or raisins)
- 100g walnuts, roughly chopped, plus a few broken ones for decoration
- 1 tbsp grated orange zest (save some to the side for decoration)

For the icing

- 80g cashews, soaked in cold water for 2 hours
- 1 tbsp maple syrup
- 1 tsp vanilla extract
- 3–4 tbsp milk
- juice of 1 lemon
- pinch of ground cinnamon

Preheat the oven to 180°C. Line and grease a 21.5 x 11 x 7cm loaf tin. I like to use brown paper bags that I have left over instead of shop-bought baking parchment – it works just as well.

In a large bowl, mix the flour, baking powder, cinnamon, nutmeg, ginger and salt until evenly combined and set aside. In another bowl, stir together the apple sauce, milk, vanilla extract, coconut oil and maple syrup. Gently pour the wet mixture over the dry ingredients and fold together. Add the carrots, dates, walnuts and orange zest.

Tip the batter into the lined tin and bake for 40–50 minutes. Stick a knife in the centre after 40 minutes; when it comes out clean – it's ready! Remove the cake from the oven and set aside to cool completely.

While the cake is baking, make the icing. Drain the cashews and add them to a blender with the maple syrup, vanilla, milk, lemon juice and cinnamon and blend until smooth and silky. Place in the fridge to thicken – it will take about 40 minutes, the time the cake is in the oven.

Once cool, remove the cake from the tin and peel off any paper. Place on a board or plate, then tip the icing on to the centre, smoothing it out to the sides with the back of a spoon. Scatter over the walnuts and orange zest before serving.

MAKES 12

SWEET AND CREAMY PEANUT BUTTER CHOCOLATE CUPS

Chocolate and nut butter complement each other so well, like my favourite childhood sandwich, peanut butter and jelly or crumpets and butter.

I grew up in the land of Reese's peanut butter cups, so this concoction has an element of nostalgia, without the added sugar and of course, plastic. What's more, these sweet and creamy cups don't require any parchment paper.

- 2 tbsp coconut oil
- 7 tbsp chocolate chips (you can find them package-free in bulk stores)
- 2 tsp vanilla extract
- 3 tbsp coconut nectar
- 300g peanut butter
- coarse salt, to decorate

For a crunchy topping (optional)

- small handful of buckwheat groats or puffed quinoa

Set a small heatproof bowl over a saucepan of simmering water (the double boil process, see page 130), making sure the bowl doesn't touch the water or the chocolate will overheat and split. Keep over a low heat and add 1 tablespoon of the coconut oil. Next, add the chocolate chips and begin to mix, allowing the chocolate to melt. Now add the vanilla extract, half the coconut nectar and fold the ingredients together. Remove from the heat and leave to cool for 2–3 minutes before pouring all but a few tablespoons of the chocolate into a 12-hole cupcake tray (I use a silicone one with indents to give the edges of the cups a nice finish and make them easy to remove). Place the tray in the freezer to set the chocolate while you melt the peanut butter.

Using the same saucepan of heated water, set another heatproof bowl on top and melt the remaining tablespoon of coconut oil. Once melted remove from thhe heat and add the peanut butter. Mix well and fold in the remaining vanilla extract and coconut nectar.

continued on page 136 . . .

Remove the cupcake tray from the freezer and pour the melted peanut butter on top of the chocolate. If you want to get fancy and have fun with your sweet treat, add a teaspoon of the remaining chocolate to the tops of your cups and use a fork to pull the chocolate into a fun design. If you want an added crunch, add a few pieces of buckwheat groats or puffed quinoa to the centre of each one.

Place the cupcake tray in the freezer for 10–15 minutes, or until the cups are completely hard. To remove, flip the tray over on to a clean surface. They should pop right out.

Add a pinch of salt to the top of each one and serve immediately, or store in a sealed container in a freezer for up to a 3 weeks – though it will be hard to not finish them all before then!

MAKES 12 COOKIES AND ABOUT 750G NICE CREAM

COCONUT BANANA NICE CREAM AND CHOCOLATE CHIP COOKIES

Even though my father was the chef, my mother would always allow me to help her bake desserts in the kitchen on the weekends. Whenever she decided to bake, I was always there, sneakily waiting for her to pass me the empty bowl to lick clean of whatever remained. Not an easy feat when you have three siblings.

Cookies and ice cream are, I believe, the greatest combination in a dessert, ever. What's better than that is putting them together to make an ice cream sandwich. The only ice cream sandwiches I ever had when I was a kid were from the neighbourhood ice cream truck and they were always in plastic wrap. Times have changed, no more chasing after the ice-cream truck; I can make my own. This is truly the best combination – the cool creaminess of ice cream and the soft chewiness of cookies – my death row dessert, for sure.

For the coconut banana nice cream

120ml canned coconut cream, frozen in an ice-cube tray

4 ripe bananas, rouchly chopped and frozen

1 tsp maple syrup

pinch of salt

For the cookies

300g plain flour

1 tsp salt

1 tsp bicarbonate of soda

1 tsp baking powder

100g virgin coconut oil, solid

100g soft dark or light brown sugar

1 tbsp vanilla extract

50ml coconut milk (from the coconut can)

100g dark chocolate chips or a 100g bar, chopped into 5mm pieces

1 tbsp coconut oil

To start, begin by placing your frozen coconut cream, bananas, maple syrup and salt in a blender or food processor and blend on a low speed for a few seconds. This may require you to stop every few seconds to mix by hand and release the frozen bits that stick to the walls. If you have a hand blender, this may be easier. You want to keep the frozen consistency, so resist adding any liquid and all will work out perfectly.

Keep blending until the frozen mixture is the consistency of a thick, soft-serve ice cream, then transfer to a bowl and place in the freezer for 25–30 minutes.

continued on page 139. . .

On to the cookies. Preheat the oven to 190°C. Have two big bowls ready.

Add the dry ingredients (flour, salt, baking soda and powder) to one bowl and whisk with a fork a couple times to break it up and mix everything evenly. Place the bowl to the side.

Add the coconut oil and sugar to the other bowl and begin to mash and mix the two together. This may take a few minutes. Once the sugar and coconut oil combine you'll have a thick sugary paste. Add your vanilla extract and milk and mix together.

Now, add your dry ingredients to the wet and fold all the ingredients together. Get your hands in there to bring it all together. Just before the mixture starts to look like dough, add half the dark chocolate chips, or chopped pieces, and mix into a ball of dough.

Using your hand, scoop out a palm-sized amount of dough and roll it into a ball with both hands then place on a baking tray. The balls need to have lots of room between them – about 7–10cm (the size of your fist). Press each ball down lightly. Bake in the oven for 12–14 minutes until light brown on top and around the edges and the centre is baked through, then remove from the oven and set aside to cool completely.

When you're ready to serve, take the ice cream out of the freezer and allow it to thaw a little before scooping, if needed. Don't wait too long as the ice cream will melt quickly. Make sure it is still solid but easy enough to scoop. Sandwich the cookies together with ice cream and freeze again for 15–20 minutes to firm up.

Meanwhile melt the remaining chocolate. Set a small heatproof bowl over a saucepan of simmering water, making sure the bowl doesn't touch the water or the chocolate will overheat and split. Keep over a low heat and add the tablespoon of coconut oil. Next, add the chocolate chips and begin to mix, allowing the chocolate to melt. Dip each cookie sandwich into the melted chocolate and serve immediately, or store in the freezer in an airtight container for up 3 days.

TIP

Use the leftover coconut milk from the can to make your own yoghurt (see page 38), replacing the cashews for coconut, or place in a container, freeze and use for curry later in the week (see page 108 for my recipe).

HOW YOUR FOOD CHOICES IMPACT THE ENVIRONMENT

The food we eat doesn't magically appear on shelves. It had to come from somewhere. There are factors involved in putting bread on your table or oat milk in your latte and this all has an impact on our environment. Water usage, energy, transportation, labour, land, waste, packaging and so much more goes into the production and distribution of our food and this all pays a price on our planet. Let's take a look and see the impact our food has on our planet.

IF YOU HAVE 1–2 AVOCADOS PER WEEK

Over a year your consumption of avocados is contributing 15kg to your annual greenhouse gas emissions.

» That's the equivalent of driving a regular petrol car 39 miles (65km)

» the same as heating the average UK home for 2 days

» using 3.519 litres of water, equal to 54 showers lasting 8 minutes

IF YOU HAVE BREAD 3–5 TIMES A WEEK

[1 SLICE PER SERVING]

Over an entire year your consumption of bread is contributing 12kg to your annual greenhouse gas emissions. That's equivalent to:

» driving a regular petrol car 32 miles (51km)
» heating the average UK home for 2 days
» using 5,140 litres of water, equal to 79 showers lasting 8 minutes.

IF YOU HAVE DARK CHOCOLATE 1–2 TIMES A WEEK

[1 CHOCOLATE BAR PER SERVING]

» Over an entire year your consumption of chocolate is contributing 116kg to your annual greenhouse gas emissions, equivalent to driving 296 miles (476km); heating your home for 18 days; using 1937 litres of water, equal to 29 showers lasting 8 minutes

IF YOU HAVE OAT MILK ONCE A DAY

[1 GLASS (200ML) PER SERVING]

Over a year this will contribute 65kg greenhouse gas emissions, equivalent to:

» driving 168 miles (270km)
» using 3,512 litres of water, equal to 54 showers of 8 minutes

IF YOU HAVE COW'S MILK ONCE A DAY

[1 GLASS (200ML) PER SERVING]

Over a year this contributes 229kg to your annual greenhouse gas emissions, equivalent to:

- » driving 585 miles (941km)
- » 36 days of heating your home
- » 45,733 litres of water, equal to 703 showers lasting 8 minutes

IF YOU HAVE PEAS 3–5 TIMES A WEEK

[80G PER SERVING]

Over a year this contributes 3kg to your annual greenhouse gas emissions, equivalent to:

- » driving 9 miles (15km)
- » 0.6 days heating the average UK home

IF YOU HAVE CHEESE ONCE A DAY

[30G PER SERVING, ENOUGH TO COVER TWO CRACKERS]

Over a year this contributes 3,352kg greenhouse gas emissions, equivalent to:

- » driving a car 899 miles (1,447km)
- » 55 days of heating a UK hhome
- » 82,703 litres of water or 1,272 showers of 8 minutes

IF YOU HAVE TOFU 1–2 TIMES A WEEK

[75G PER SERVING, EQUIVALENT TO TWO LAMB CHOPS]

Over a year this contributes 339kg to your annual greenhouse gas emissions, equivalent to:

» driving 865 miles (1,392km)

» 1 return flight from London to Malaga

IF YOU HAVE BEER ONCE A DAY

[1 PINT PER SERVING]

Over a year this contributes 243kg to your annual greenhouse gas emissions, equivalent to:

» driving 622 miles (1,002km)

» 38 days of heating a UK home

» 3,535 litres of water, equal to 54 showers lasting 8 minutes

HOW MUCH IMPACT DOES FOOD HAVE?

» A quarter of global emissions come from food

» More than half of food emissions come from animal products

» Half of all farmed animal emissions come from just beef and lamb.

Avoiding meat and dairy products is one of the biggest ways to reduce your environmental impact, according to recent scientific studies. But knowing how and where your food is produced is also important, as the same food can have huge differences in environmental impact. Changing your diet can make a big difference to your personal environmental footprint, from saving water to reducing pollution and the loss of forests.

Source: https://www.bbc.co.uk/news/science-environment-46459714, accessed 29 May 2019

SERVES 4–6

OAT PULP RASPBERRY CRUMBLE

You've started making your own oat milk from scratch and now you are wondering what to do with the leftover pulp? I think you're getting the hang of this 'no-waste mindset' – congratulations!

This recipe is so easy to prepare and requires little effort – you'll be amazed by the yummy result. You can also use any other nut or seed milk pulp you have left over in place of the oat pulp.

- 230g rhubarb, cut into 1cm pieces
- 165g raspberries, fresh or frozen
- 1 tbsp maple syrup
- grated zest and juice of 1 lemon
- 2½ tsp cornflour
- 85g oats (rolled or jumbo – use whatever you have)
- 25g desiccated coconut
- 100g leftover oat pulp from making oat milk (see page 194)
- 2 tsp baking powder
- 60g soft brown sugar
- ¼ tsp ground cinnamon
- 240g plain flour
- 20–40g coconut oil
- ¼ tsp salt

To serve

- coconut yoghurt

Combine the rhubarb, raspberries, maple syrup, lemon zest and juice in a saucepan over a medium heat. Bring to a vigorous boil, stirring, then let it simmer for 8–10 minutes. Add the cornflour half a teaspoon at a time, stirring until dissolved. Let the fruit cook for 2–3 minutes more until thickened. Remove from the heat and allow to cool for 10 minutes.

Preheat your oven to 180°C.

Place the oats and all the remaining ingredients in a large bowl, and mix until combined. You may need to add a bit more oats or shredded coconut if the mixture is too wet – it should be thick and spreadable.

Pack half the oat mixture into a 22cm baking tin or dish (circular or square is fine). Bake in the oven for 10 minutes, or until the crust is lightly brown. Remove from oven and allow it to cool for 10 minutes.

Top the crust with the fruit mixture, then sprinkle the top with the rest of the oat mixture. Bake for another 20–25 minutes, or until the topping is lightly browned. Remove from the heat and serve with a spoonful of coconut yoghurt.

SERVES 4

BANANA SPLITS

It's a shame that we don't appreciate food at all its stages. We are programmed to like the beautiful, firm yellow banana in the supermarket, and in doing so, we end up wasting countless bananas every year – it is the most wasted fruit in the world. But your spotty and bruised bananas are good to use and should always be eaten – they're perfect for this simple 5-minute recipe.

4 ripe bananas, peeled nad frozen whole (see tip)
120g nut butter
2 dates, pitted and finely chopped
25g dark chocolate, melted
35g Banana bread granola (see page 36)
115g berries
115g coconut flakes

To serve
Ice cream
yoghurt

Removel the bananas from the freezer.

Put the nut butter, dates and chocolate into a food processor and pulse until you have a smooth, thick sauce.

Put the bananas on to a plate and drizzle them with your sauce. Top with granola, berries and coconut flakes. If you have a bit of ice cream or yoghurt this would be a lovely addition.

TIP

Freeze the bananas an hour before you want to serve this so that they are slightly chilled and firm.

MAKES 12–14

NOTHING WASTED BOUNTY TRUFFLES

This recipe has been a long time coming. I made tens of thousands of hand-made chocolates when I worked as a chocolatier in Australia. There was something really beautiful about the repetitiveness of making and cooking the truffles, enjoying every moment.

This is a no-bake treat and ready within a few short minutes. I like using my hands to mix and make them as it brings you a little closer to your food and gives you a connection. Enjoy with a cuppa after a long day, but be sure to not eat them all at once.

135g desiccated coconut

2 tbsp coconut oil, soft or melted

35ml coconut milk (see page 194 for how to make your own)

1½ tsp maple syrup or coconut nectar

salt

40g dark chocolate

To decorate (optional)

crushed nuts

chopped candied citrus fruit

chopped dried fruit

Use your hands for this! In a separate bowl mix your desiccated coconut, 1 tablespoon coconut oil and milk until the ingredients are thoroughly combined. Next, add your maple syrup and a pinch of salt and continue to mix. If mixture is wet, add more coconut until the mixture has the consistency of a thick cookie dough.

To form truffles, scoop a teaspoon of the coconut mixture and roll it in the centre of your hands. Begin to shape the mixture into small balls and place on a chopping board or plate. Once finished, place into the freezer for 10 minutes while you melt the chocolate.

Place 3–5cm of water in a small saucepan and bring to a simmer. Fit a heatproof bowl over the top making sure the bottom doesn't touch the water. Add the chocolate, remaining tablespoon of coconut oil and a pinch of salt and begin to stir. The mixture will begin to melt. Once there are a few solid pieces of chocolate left you can remove from heat and allow the melted mixture to cool.

TIP

These are perfect to save and keep in a sealed container in your fridge for 5 days or in your freezer for up to 1 month.

Remove from the freezer and drop a coconut ball in the bowl of warm chocolate, covering it completely. Using two forks, scoop the coconut out of the chocolate and allow any access to drip off. Place back on to a cutting board or plate and once you've coated all the balls, freeze for another 10–15 minutes.

If you want to decorate your truffles, add a few bits of crushed nuts, candied citrus peel, or chopped dried fruit to the warm chocolate before dipping the coconut balls in it. The balls can be kept in the freezer for up to 1 month.

MAKES 12

STUFFED DATES

My favourite thing to do in the kitchen besides cooking or baking is restocking my cupboard – I'm constantly visiting a bulk or zero-waste store with package-free ingredients to refill my jars and containers. The three ingredients that I go through the most are typically dates, nut butter and chocolate.

I'm not the biggest fan of chocolate by itself and think chocolate always needs a supporting character or two, but I know that most people love it. What I love to do is combine these three kitchen essentials. The best part of this is you can make a big batch and freeze them so that there's always a little treat ready for you.

- 12 Medjool dates, pitted
- 6 tsp nut butter
- 1 x 100g bar of dark chocolate, finely chopped
- sprinkle of sea salt

Press the centre of the pitted date to create space for the nut butter. Stuff half a teaspoon of nut butter into each date. A pinch of salt makes this go from yum to woah!

Melt your chocolate (see page 130) and dip the suffed date and nut butter into it. Place on a plate and freeze for 15–20 minutes, then store in the freezer in a sealed container for 1 week.

ZERO WASTE FOR YOUR SKIN AND BODY

LAVENDER AND ROSEMARY BODY SCRUB

Our skin is our body's largest organ and taking care of it is a lot of work. If we look at what we are eating and putting into our bodies then we should look at what we are putting onto our bodies too. Here is a simple and easy natural body scrub – say goodbye to plastic beauty products.

6 tbsp sugar
3 tsp soft coconut oil
1 tsp dried rosemary
10 drops of lavender essential oil (or another oil you like)

In a bowl, mix your sugar and coconut oil until it becomes a wet and gritty paste. Then add the dried rosemary and essential oil and mix well. Keep your body scrub in a sealed container in a cool dry space. Use on dry or damp skin in the shower. Rub in circular motions over your body, especially in the dry areas, like elbows and knees. Rinse off with warm water and feel your skin come to life.

AVOCADO LEMON FACE MASK

We live in a world with constant notifications, endless to-do lists and all those open tabs rattling in your mind, but seriously, how did you forget that you had a half-eaten avocado sitting in your fridge? Let's make use for what we have and find alternative ways to get the best of what we might typically discard. This requires a little shift in mindset, a bit of effort, but will reward you with a hydrated and refreshing face.

½ avocado
juice of ½ lemon
1 tbsp coconut oil

Combine and mash the ingredients in a bowl until you have a smooth and creamy paste that will stick to your face. Apply to your face and neck. Sit back and relax for 10–15 minutes, then rinse off with warm water and feel alive again.

COFFEE SCRUB

We all need a good exfoliator, so why not choose one with natural properties to buff away your dry skin? A coffee scrub will help eliminate dead skin cells while working with your body's natural renewal process to help produce new ones. This is a natural way to avoid the pollution that can be created by shop-bought products as well as being a great way to upcycle your coffee grounds. Enjoy your morning coffee scrub while you sip on your cup of joe in the shower – you multitasker, you!

3 tbsp coffee grounds (ideally used)
about 1 tbsp sugar
1 tbsp natural oil of your choice: olive, grape seed, coconut, or almond

Mix the coffee and sugar, then add the oil. Based on the kind of scrub consistency you want, add more or less brown sugar. Using circular motions, gently massage on to your body - paying close attention to areas that are prone to dryness (elbows, knees, backs of arms) and then rinse with warm water. (Your bath or shower may need a little scrub afterwards too).

If you're putting this on your face, take special care, especially around the sensitive eye area.

TOOTHPASTE WITHOUT THE PLASTIC TUBE

After I went plastic-free and my plastic tube of toothpaste ran out, I was left to create my own from scratch. And guess what? All my teeth remain. Please note, I am not a dentist, but I really want you to create less waste: imagine how many tubes of toothpaste end up in landfill each year? I'm going to guess a lot. Fresh homemade toothpaste in 2 minutes, are you ready?

70g coconut oil
1 tbsp coarse salt
1 tbsp calcium carbonate
100g bicarbonate of soda
½ tsp liquid stevia
10 drops of peppermint oil

Place all the ingredients in a bowl and mash well– if you have a pestle and mortar, this can be used too. The result should be smooth and have a paste-like consistency. Store in a sterilised sealed container to avoid any bacterial growth and use a clean spoon to get the paste on to your brush to avoid contaminating to your container. Use within 6 months.

DIY DEODORANT ⊕

If I told you can smell lovely and save money would you believe me? Well, this do-it-yourself deodorant is the one for you. The simple recipe is easy to put together and feels more natural than rubbing on some manufactured pour-clogging deodorant.

4 tsp bicarbonate of soda or arrow root
5 tsp soft coconut oil
5–10 drops essential oil
small mason jar

Put the bicarbonate of soda and coconut oil into a bowl and mix well, then add 5–10 drops of essential oils, depending on the strength of the oil and how strong you want your deodorant to smell. Place in a small mason jar and store in a dark and cool area. Apply by scooping out a quarter of a teaspoon with a spoon. Rub it together in both hands and apply to your armpits. Keep store, sealed in a cool dark cupboard or fridge for 6 months.

05

MAKE IT FROM SCRATCH

COOKING DRIED PULSES AND BEANS

I absolutely love the enjoyment I get from cooking my pulses from scratch. This was most likely the way our grandparents would cook back when there weren't tinned beans at our convenience.

So, how do we prepare pulses from scratch? First, for the purposes of shopping with less plastic waste, visit a bulk shop where you can pick up what's available to you. Rinse your pulses with water to remove any debris that may be lingering from the bulk bin or from how it was transferred to the shop.

Place your rinsed pulses in a bowl and add triple the amount of boiling water – i.e. 100g pulses to 300ml water. Cover with a plate to keep in the heat. Soak your pulses for up to 24 hours or until they are soft and squeezable.

The next day, discard the soaking water, place the pulses in a sieve and rinse well under cold running water. This will wash away any carbohydrates responsible for flatulence.

The following chart gives approximate times in rough order of size, from small or split to large. Cooking times also depend on the age of the beans. Properly cooked beans should be tender but not too mushy.

PULSE	SOAKING TIME	COOKING TIME
Split lentils	No soaking required	15–20 minutes
Split peas	Minimum 2 hours	30–35 minutes
Brown or green lentils	2 Hours Unsoaked	20–30 minutes 25–40 minutes
Mung or aduki bean	Minimum 2 hours	25–40 minutes
Black-eyed bean	6–8 Hours or overnight	30–60 minutes
Kidney beans	6–8 Hours or overnight	1–1¼ hours
Cannellini/pinto /black beans	Overnight	1–1 ½ hours
Chickpeas	Overnight	1–1½ hours
Soya beans	Minimum 12 hours	1½–3 hours

4–6 SERVINGS

PLASTIC-FREE PASTA

As a child, I remember my mother making homemade pasta from scratch almost every Saturday morning. It was such a treat to have a home-cooked meal – especially when made completely from scratch. Not only is making your own pasta delicious and fun, it also reduces the amount of single-use plastic that, sadly, the majority of shop-bought pasta is wrapped in. All ingredients can be purchased at a bulk shop to make it zero waste.

325g semolina flour
130g plain flour
pinch of salt
180ml warm water
1 tbsp olive oil

To serve (optional)
olive oil
grated lemon zest
black pepper
crisp fried sage leaves (see page 70)

TIP

Cut the dough in half and freeze in an airtight container for up to one month.

Begin by mixing the semolina, flour and salt together in a big bowl. Slowly add your warm water while mixing with the flour. Next, add your olive oil. Begin to knead your dough, pressing the heel of your palm into the dough, then folding the dough back towards you. You may have some flour left over at the bottom of the bowl and that is totally okay, you will use it later. Just be sure that you get most of it and keep those hands moving by kneading the dough. After about 3–5 minutes of kneading, take the dough out of the bowl and knead on a floured work surface for 1 more minute. You want a smooth ball of dough. Now, give the dough some tough love by throwing it down onto your work surface. After a minute, put the ball of dough into a lightly floured bowl and cover with a tea towel.

Allow the dough to rest for at least 30 minutes, or up to 1 hour. At this point, the pasta dough could be refrigerated for up to 24 hours. Let it come back to room temperature before rolling. During this resting time, the water will be absorbed by the flour and the gluten strands will relax, which will give you a strong and rollable dough.

Take your dough out of the bowl and place it on a floured surface. If you want to freeze some dough – cut it in half and do it at this point. If you have a pasta machine, pass the dough through the widest setting on the machine. Keep rolling it until

it's nice and shiny. If you're not using a pasta machine, roll your pasta on a lightly floured surface with a rolling pin. Roll the dough gently from the centre outwards, but remember not to apply added pressure – your rolling should be soft and gentle or you'll have thinner spots in the dough. Roll the dough until it is like a thin and slightly transparent paper (if you feel the dough is sticking, lightly flour the dough). To cut the pasta, you can use a pasta machine or work your knife skills. I use a pizza cutter to cut each piece of dough into thick fettuccine-sized noodles. You can rest the pasta for a second time (30 minutes–1 hour) or cook it immediately. If you decide to wait, the dough will become a bit more dried and sturdier.

Bring a saucepan of water to the boil. Add a pinch of salt to the boiling water – then add your pasta next. The pasta will cook quickly – within 2–3 minutes. Check it's cooked by tasting a strand.

Serve with your sauce of choice or just with a drizzle of olive oil, some lemon zest, black pepper and crispy sage – yum!

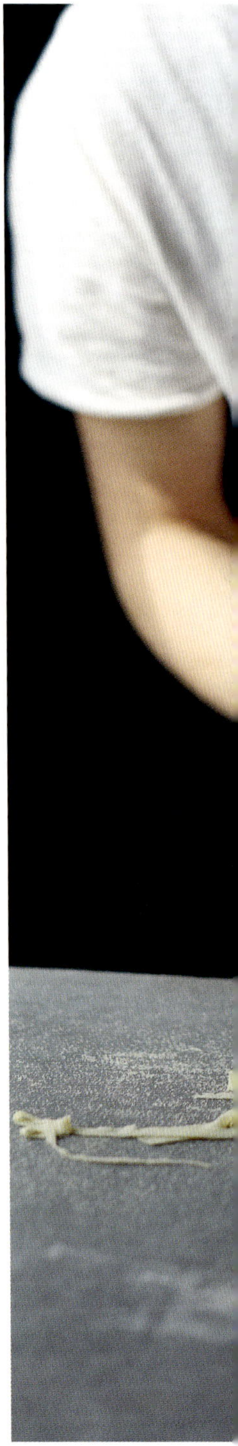

RICE IT OR SPIRALISE IT

Pasta is my spirit animal, but spiralised and riced veggies come a close second.

RICE IT	SPIRALISE IT
Take your chosen vegetable and grate it using a grater. You can use any hole size you'd like, but I prefer the largest holes for grating for thick pieces.	*Either spiralise the veg using a spiraliser, but don't worry if you don't own one, you can still make fancy-looking noodles without the equipment. Peel the vegetables in long ribbons with a vegetable peeler, the more pressure you add to peeling the thicker the vegetable slices will be.* *Enjoy the ribbons as they are, or cut them into thin strips for noodles.*
Beetroot, broccoli, butternut squash, carrot, cauliflower, courgette, daikon, parsnip, plantain, Romanesco, sweet potato, turnip and yellow squash.	Apple, beetroot, broccoli stalks, butternut squash, carrot, celeriac, courgette, cucumber, daikon, melon, onion, parsnip, pear, pepper, potato, radish, sweet potato, turnip, yellow squash.

SOME IDEAS FOR WHAT TO DO WITH YOUR RICE AND NOODLES:

» Broccoli rice makes an awesome base for a bowl; sauté it lightly in oil with salt and pepper.

» Beetroot noodles or rice make a great side: have it raw or sauté it with ginger and garlic.

» Cauliflower rice is great lightly sautéed with salt and pepper in sesame oil.

» Red pepper noodles make a colourful addition to a salad.

» Apple noodles make a gorgeous dessert – try drizzling melted chocolate over them (you're welcome).

» Radish spirals make a pretty garnish for salads and tacos.

» Sweet potato noodles are a great alternative for pasta and good in stir-fries.

» Courgette ribbons are great raw in a salad or even in warm stew.

SERVES 4

HOW TO ROAST VEGGIES LIKE A PRO

Some of my favourite dinners are just very simply roasted vegetables. It's so quick and easy to chop them up and toss them in the oven, but the result is always spot on.

This is a great way to use up food that is lingering. What about that sweet potato you haven't touched in 2 weeks? Or that courgette that is softening in the fridge? And what about that half-eaten red pepper that you said you would finish? We are all busy, but throwing food isn't smart financially or environmentally.

Bonus round, there's minimal cleaning up to do. Winner-winner (no-chicken) dinner.

MAIN VEGETABLE (CHOOSE 1)

1 butternut squash, roughly chopped, 2–3 sweet potatoes, roughly chopped, 3–4 parsnips, roughly chopped, 3 fennel bulbs, cut into wedges

+

SUPPORTING VEGETABLE (CHOOSE 2)

1 red onion, cut into wedges, 2 red peppers, roughly chopped, 1 leek, chopped, 10–15 Brussels sprouts (all leaves included), 3–4 carrots, roughly chopped, 2–3 tomatoes, cut into quarters

+

SMALL, BUT HEARTY (CHOOSE 1)

200g dried chickpeas, soaked and cooked, 200g dried kidney beans, soaked and cooked, 140g garden peas

+

TO FINISH

a light drizzle of oil, stale bread, torn into chunks (optional), paprika, salt and pepper

+

TO SERVE

fresh herbs, chopped or grated lemon zest

Preheat your oven to 220°C. Put all your chosen vegetables into a baking tray. Drizzle over a small amount of oil to coat them and season with salt, pepper and paprika.

Roast in the oven for 30–35 minutes, until the vegetables are soft and golden. If you're adding pulses or peas to the tray, add them for the last 10–15 minutes, mixing them well. If you have any uneaten or leftover bread add it for the last 8–10 minutes. Remove from the oven and finish the vegetables by scattering them with a chopped herb or lemon zest.

Serve your roasted veggies as a side to a main or completely on their own as a simple lunch or dinner.

SERVES 1 – EASILY SCALED UP

HOW TO MAKE A KICK-ASS SALAD AND WASTE LESS FOOD

For those who doubt the power and deliciousness of a huge hearty salad, this one's for you. It may seem boring and uneventful to create a salad, but this is a creative way to get rid of unwanted or uneaten fruit and vegetables.

Choose your leafy base, veggies, crunch, herbs (and bulk it out with a portion of rice, quinoa or lentils if you're feeling hungry).

Serve your salad up in a big bowl, drizzle on your favourite dressing (to taste) and mix it all up. If you're eating alone, why not create enough for two portions? Simply store in the fridge in an airtight sealed container for a leftovers lunch or as a side salad for your dinner, it should keep nicely for 1-2 days and you can always freshen it up with some extra bits.

START WITH A LEAFY BASE (2–3 HANDFULS PER PERSON)

leftover spinach, rocket, shredded kale or spring greens, radicchio, endive, baby gem lettuce, broccoli, sprouts,

+

EAT YOUR VEGGIES (1 HANDFUL PER PERSON)

pickled cabbage that's sitting in your fridge, tomatoes, ½ avocado, sliced, radishes, spiralised/ribboned courgette (see page 166), grated carrot, roasted vegetables (see page. 171)

+

ADD SOME CRUNCH (1 HANDFUL PER PERSON)

toasted breadcrumbs, seeds, nuts, apple

+

TOP WITH HERBS (1 SMALL HANDFUL PER PERSON)

carrot tops, celery leaves, beetroot leaves, leftover mint, unwanted coriander, forgotten dill

+

THE FINAL TOUCH (TO TASTE)

drizzle with olive oil, squeeze of ½ lemon, balsamic or white wine vinegar, salt, pepper, chilli flakes

MAKES 3–4 SERVINGS, AS A SNACK

OVEN-BAKED BEETROOT

This vegetable is so versatile and yet so often undervalued. Make those unwanted beetroot into some amazing crisps for an easy afternoon snack.

- 6–8 medium assorted beetroot
- 1 tbsp olive oil
- 1 tsp flaky salt, plus extra to finish
- ½ tsp black pepper, plus extra to finish
- chopped herbs, such as rosemary, thyme, parsley, chives, sage

Preheat your oven to 190°C.

Use a mandolin or a sharp knife to slice the beetroot as thinly as you can. Toss with the olive oil, salt and pepper.

Place beetroot on two separate baking trays and give them some space to bake – no overcrowding please. Bake until crisp, about 15–20 minutes. Toss your warm beet chips in flaky salt, black pepper and the herbs.

MAKES ABOUT 500ML

FOOD WASTE VEGETABLE STOCK

The question I get asked the most is 'What can I do with my vegetable tops and tails, odds and ends?'. This is the recipe that solves this problem. Not only are you not wasting food you're also eliminating single use plastic.

Here's a tip – every time you cook from now on, place a bowl beside your cutting board. Any trimmings that don't go towards cooking go into the bowl. Save these scraps in a bowl in your freezer. Once you have about 2–4 cups of food scraps you're ready to make your stock.

ends of onions and skins, even garlic cloves

carrot peelings

potato skins

those unwanted Brussels sprout leaves

broccoli that has seen better days

any part of the celery

that green stem of a pepper

beetroot leaves

cauliflower core and leaves

soft mushrooms

banged up tomatoes

wilted leafy greens that are done for

herbs that were never used

Put your vegetable scraps into a big saucepan, and pour in enough water to cover your scraps (around 700ml).

Bring to the boil and leave to simmer for 30–40 minutes. You'll know it's ready when the vegetables have wilted and are soft and the liquid has turned a slightly darker colour and gives off an earthy aroma.

Strain the food scraps and collect the liquid. Fill containers with your homemade vegetable stock and store in jars in your fridge for up to 1 week or in freezable containers in your freezer for 1 month.

MAKES 120G

AQUAFABA BUTTER

Notice how most butter products in the supermarket are packaged in plastic? This butter is planet-friendly and a delicious way to use that leftover water from soaking chickpeas, or from the can.

Chickpea water is a really useful ingredient and can be made into delicious things like meringue and marzipan. Scientifically, it's known as 'aquafaba' – a joining of the Latin words 'water' and 'bean'. I'll save you from the history lesson so you can get started on making your own. Note that you should sterilise your cooking equipment in boiling water first to prolong the life of your butter.

- 75g virgin coconut oil
- 4 tsp rapeseed or olive oil
- 3 tbsp aquafaba (chickpea water)
- ½ tsp salt
- 1½ tsp nutritional yeast
- ¾ tsp Apple scrap vinegar (see page 192) or lemon juice

TIP

For whipped butter, transfer your desired amount into a bowl and with a hand whisk or stick blender slowly begin to whip until you're satisfied with the consistency.

Melt the coconut oil in a saucepan over a medium heat. Remove from the heat and allow it to cool for a moment. Add the rapeseed oil and stir, then leave the mixture to cool to room temperature.

Add the aquafaba, salt, nutritional yeast and vinegar to a bowl and start blending with a stick blender. While the blender is running, add your oil slowly, making sure that the oil is incorporated throughout before adding any more.

The consistency should begin to thicken nicely once all the oil is added. Place the bowl in a deep dish of ice and continue to blend. The ice surrounding the bowl will help with the thickening of the oils. Once thickened to the consistency of a mayo or aioli, remove and place in a sterilised jar. Place a small cloth over the opening and leave in your fridge for up to 6 hours. Once it hardens, seal the jar and keep in the fridge for up to 7 days.

MAKES 250G

SAY 'CHEESE' EVERYONE

When you ask people who have switched to a plant-based diet about the thing they miss the most, the majority will say 'cheese' – myself included. No more cheese pizza, no more grated Parmesan on a big bowl of spaghetti, no more Brie, feta, halluomi – what was I going to do? I started experimenting with how to make simple plant-based equivalents in my kitchen. Maybe it doesn't have the chew of halloumi, or the scent of feta, but it still gives me the greatest pleasure to whip up a quick cheese sauce. There are only a few ingredients that you'll need to make a cheese sauce, which can go on practically anything. Elevate your salads and roasted veg with this homemade cheese sauce, or even serve it as a dip.

START WITH A NUT OR SEED BASE (CHOOSE 1)

100g cashews, almonds, hazelnut, walnuts or pumpkin seeds, soaked in boiling water (for an hour or more) then rinsed

+

ADD SOME OIL

2 tbsp extra virgin olive oil, rapeseed oil or sunflower oil

+

CHOOSE A LIQUID

35ml water, coconut milk, oat milk or vegetable stock

+

ADD SOME ACIDITY

1 tbsp lime juice, lemon juice or apple cider vinegar

+

ADD FLAVOUR

pinch of black pepper, agave, cumin, paprika, garlic or Italian seasoning

+

ADD A HERB (OPTIONAL)

parsley, thyme, sage, dill, fennel fronds, basil, or coriander

+

ADD A RAW OR ROASTED VEGETABLE (OPTIONAL)

red peppers, carrots, kale or courgette

+

FINISH WITH

20g nutritional yeast

Combine your chosen ingredients in a food processor and blend for 1–2 minutes until smooth and creamy. Add in a little water to loosen if necessary.

Pour over your favourite salads, use as a side for roasted veg or drizzle over pizza. You'll find any reason to get this cheesy sauce all over your food.

TIP

Perfect with my veggie burgers on page 118!

MAKES 1 x 900G LOAF

BREAD

I don't know what it is with bread, but I absolutely love it. It might have to do with growing up around my father's restaurants and smelling the freshly baked bread being made every single day. Homemade bread is nothing like the bread you buy at a supermarket. I love adding chopped herb stems to the dough just before it goes in the oven to give it a different, fresher dimension.

- ¾ tsp dried active yeast
- 200ml warm water
- 1 tbsp caster sugar
- 260g plain flour, sifted, plus extra for dusting
- 1 tsp salt
- leftover chopped thyme or rosemary stalks, chopped (optional)
- extra virgin olive oil, for drizzling

Put your yeast, warm water and sugar into a bowl and whisk rapidly. Bubbles should start to form and foam. Whisk for 1–2 minutes, then set aside to rest.

Put your sifted flour and salt into a separate bowl.

Pour your wet solution slowly into the bowl of flour and begin to mix and fold it with your hands. Continue to fold and combine your water solution and flour. The dough will start out quite wet, but as you continue to mix in the flour it will become drier. Sprinkle with a bit of flour, if necessary, to help the process.

Begin to knead the dough using the heel of your palm and repeat for 4–5 minutes. Remove the dough from the bowl and place on a floured surface.

Continuing to knead, sprinkle a bit more flour over the dough; it should start to feel smooth and soft.

Put the dough back in a clean, dry bowl, sprinkle over a bit more flour and cover with a tea towel. Place the dough an incubated space (I use my oven) to prove for 1–4 hours. The longer you leave it the more bubbles and air pockets you'll have once the dough is baked.

Preheat your oven to 200°C.

Place the dough in a 900g loaf tin (about 23 x 13cm), add the herbs, if using, a light drizzle of olive oil on top and bake in the hot oven for 20–22 minutes until golden brown and the loaf sounds hollow when tapped underneath.

Serve your bread with anything. If not eaten it right away, you can store any leftover bread in the freezer – slice it first.

MAKES 6–8 NAAN

NAAN NAAN NAAN NAAN

Make your own Indian flatbread at home and never go back to plastic-wrapped shop-bought again. This is the perfect side dish for your curries or stews to soak up those leftover juices in your bowl. I think you'll be surprised at how very easy this recipe is to put together.

125ml warm water

1½ tsp dried active yeast

1 tbsp caster sugar

2 tbsp extra virgin olive oil, coconut oil or Aquafaba butter (see page 178), plus extra for frying

1 tsp salt

250g plain flour

1 tsp thyme, rosemary or sage, to garnish

In a big mixing bowl, whisk your warm water, yeast and sugar for 1–2 minutes and allow it to foam and create bubbles. If it doesn't foam, the water might be too hot and it will have killed the yeast so compost that and start over.

Once it foams, add your oil and salt and whisk briskly for another 30 seconds.

Sift your flour into a separate bowl, pour in the wet mixture little by little and begin to fold it with your hands. Knead, knead, and knead. Work that dough with the heel of your palm until it is smooth and not sticky. After a few minutes, roll and form the dough into a ball and place back in a dry floured bowl. Cover with a cloth and let it rest for 30 minutes or up to 1 hour. If you want it to be doughier and have more pockets of air, allow it to sit for the hour.

Sprinkle some flour on to a clean surface and cut the dough into 8 pieces. Press each piece of dough with your fingers to flatten it lightly. You may need a rolling pin to stretch it out.

Add 1 teaspoon of oil or butter to a heated frying pan. Place each piece of dough in the heated frying pan and allow to cook for 1 minute on each side, or until golden brown around the edges. Garnish with your chosen herb.

MAKES 680G

TOMATO PURÉE

One thing I've learnt about making things from scratch is that they don't just taste like 'the real thing', they taste better. I want you never to want to purchase shop-bought tomato purée ever again.

4.5kg ripe red tomatoes, halved

2 tbsp olive oil, plus more for baking and sealing

115g agave or maple syrup or sugar

2 bay leaves

1 tbsp salt

Place the tomatoes in a medium stockpot and add the olive oil. Bring the tomatoes to a simmer, cover and cook until softened and the juices have been released – about 40–45 minutes. Remove from the heat and set aside to cool for a few minutes.

Press the tomatoes through a fine sieve or mouli to remove the skins and seeds, collecting the purée in a bowl. Return the purée to the stockpot; add the agave, bay leaves and salt. Bring to a simmer over a medium heat with the lid off and reduce until thick, stirring often, for about 50–60 minutes.

Preheat the oven to 120°C.

Grease a baking dish with about a teaspoon of oil, then spread the tomato purée out into a thin and evenly distributed layer. Bake the purée for 2½–3 hours until it becomes thick, stirring every 15–20 minutes.

Remove from the oven and cool to room temperature. Transfer the pureé to sealed sterilised jars and cover with a thin layer of olive oil. Keep in the fridge for up to 1 month.

MAKES 100G

ODDS AND ENDS PESTO

This zero-waste pesto is one of my favourite ways to re-purpose pesky green stems that would otherwise be tossed in the bin.

You can either soak your nuts in water overnight or up to 1 hour before blending.

Add the nuts or seeds to a blender. Next, add your herb stems, acidity and oil. Blend for 20–30 seconds. You may need to stop and scrap the sides of your blender. Add your flavour and blend again for 20-30 seconds or until the pesto is slightly smooth and a bit chunky.

START WITH A NUT/ SEED BASE, ABOUT 50G (CHOOSE 1)

almonds, pumpkin seeds, walnuts, pistachios, hazelnuts or pine nuts.

+

ADD THE ENDS OF HERBS, A LARGE BUNCH (OR TWO)

mint, basil, parsley, dill, coriander or marjoram

+

ADD ACIDITY (ABOUT 2 TBSP)

lime, balsamic vinegar, orange juice, rice vinegar, lemon juice, white wine vinegar

+

ADD SOME OIL (ABOUT 4 TBSP)

avocado oil, olive oil, rapeseed oil, walnut oil

+

ADD A FLAVOUR

pinch of red chilli, garlic, soy, green chilli, agave nectar, nutritional yeast

12 CRUMPETS

PLASTIC-FREE CRUMPETS

I'm quite upset and frustrated that America doesn't have anything that comes close to a crumpet. Do you remember your first crumpet? I do, and it was glorious. After my first bite, I needed crumpets in my life.

The only issue is that generally they are packaged in plastic, so I had to do some research and testing to come up with a way to make my own. I've drawn inspiration from a recipe by Delia Smith and have adapted it – mine is made all from plants, of course.

280ml milk
60ml water
1 tsp caster sugar
1 tbsp dried active yeast
230g strong plain flour
1 tsp salt
Aquafaba butter (see page 192) or coconut oil, for greasing

To serve

Aquafaba butter (see page 192)
tea!

You will need

a heavy-based frying pan and a few 8–10cm cooking rings to create that lovely crumpet shape.

Heat the milk and water in a saucepan until the liquid comes to a light simmer, but be careful not let it get too hot or it will kill the yeast. Next, pour your liquid into a mixing bowl and whisk in your sugar and dried yeast for 1 minute – it should start to foam and bubble slightly (you'll know if it's killed the yeast if there isn't foam). Leave the bowl in a warm place for 10 minutes until it is frothy on top.

In a bowl, use a fork to mix your flour and salt. Make a well in the centre using your index and middle finger and swirling them in circular motions. When the yeast mixture is frothy (and I'm sure it will be) pour it into the centre. Gradually mix the flour into the liquid, until you have a smooth, pourable batter. Cover the bowl with a tea towel and leave it in a warm place for 45 minutes–1 hour, or until the batter is frothy.

Grease the inside of the rings with butter or coconut oil– in the past I would have used paper towels with a bit of oil, now I just use my fingers and grease by hand. Grease the frying pan too. Put a few rings into the heavy-based frying pan and set it over a medium heat. When the pan is hot, pour the batter slowly into each ring so it comes a third of the way up. Leave them to cook slowly for 15 minutes. Tiny bubbles will start to appear – you need to leave the crumpets to cook until the bubbling slows down or stops. At this point remove the rings by taking a knife and sliding it in between

the crumpet and ring, flip the crumpets on to their other side and cook for 1 minute. Remove from the pan, regrease the rings and frying pan and cook the remaining batches.

Serve the crumpets warm with your homemade butter and tea. Store in a bread tin for 5 days, or properly sealed in the freezer for up to 2 weeks.

MAKE YOUR OWN CONDIMENTS

Have you ever considered making your own mouth-watering ketchup, mustard and mayo free from plastic and created from scratch? They'll taste 10 times better and will impress your friends . . . Thank me later!

MAKES 240ML

MUSTARD

- 80g yellow mustard seeds
- 45ml water
- 45ml Apple scrap cider vinegar (see page 192)
- 3 tbsp maple or agave syrup
- 2 tsp fresh lemon juice
- 1 tsp dried thyme
- ¼ tsp salt
- ¼ tsp black pepper
- ½ tsp ground turmeric

Put your mustard seeds, water and vinegar into a glass jar. Seal and refrigerate overnight.

The next afternoon, add your remaining ingredients then transfer to a blender and purée to your desired consistency. Add more maple syrup or herbs to taste.

Store in a clean, airtight glass jar in the fridge up to 4 weeks.

MAKES 400ML

KETCHUP

200g Medjool dates, pitted
200ml boiling water
170g homemade tomato purée (see page 184)
4 tbsp white vinegar or Apple scrap cider vinegar (see page 192)
1 tsp salt
2 tsp onion powder
1 tsp garlic powder
1 tsp yellow mustard seeds (powder, optinal)
pinch of ground allspice
olive oil, to store

Soak your dates in the boiling water to soften them.

Put all the other ingredients (except the oil) into a blender and blend, then slowly pour in your dates one at a time, as well as their soaking water. You may not need all the water, so slowly gauge the consistency until it's to your liking. Blend until smooth.

Pour the ketchup into a glass jar and drizzle over 1 teaspoon of olive oil to prevent the top from discolouring. Seal properly and store in your fridge for up to 4 weeks. If you don't finish it in 4 weeks, store the remainder in a suitable container in your freezer.

MAKES 210ML

MAYONNAISE

3 tbsp aquafaba (chickpea water; see page 178 for more on this)
1 tbsp fresh lemon juice
1 tsp Apple scrap vinegar (see page 192)
1 tsp maple syrup
½ tsp salt
¼ tsp mustard powder
100–140ml olive oil

Put the aquafaba, lemon juice, vinegar, maple syrup, salt and dry mustard powder into a tall container. Using a stick blender (or in jug blender), blend to combine on a low–medium speed.

While blending, slowly pour in your oil until the mixture starts to thicken and turn white and creamy. Check the seasoning. Store in an airtight container or jar and keep in the fridge for up to 2 weeks.

MAKES ABOUT 1.5 LITRES

APPLE SCRAP VINEGAR

*At this point you're probably thinking what could possibly be next? I will stop at literally nothing to prove that you can make everything from scratch – well, except maybe toilet paper because that sh*t is difficult. I also hope it's clear that we should never throw away fruit scraps with the plethora of uses there are for them!*

the peel and core from 6 large apples
1 tbsp sugar
1.5 litres water

If you don't have all the apple peel or core right now, don't worry about it – just keep them in the freezer until you have enough.

Combine all the ingredients in a large bowl, then cover with a thin cloth. Leave it somewhere at room temperature. Over the next few days, the vinegar will start to smell a bit, initially like apples and alcohol (the microbes will produce alcohol before they turn into vinegar, then the sour vinegar will develop). Stir your vinegar vigorously every day – once in the morning and once in the evening. The liquid will get frothy on top as fermentation gets going, especially when you stir it. When the colour of the liquid starts to darken, after 1–2 weeks, strain the vinegar through a colander or sieve lined with muslin (compost the apple!), then keep the vinegar at room temperature, stirring at least once a day, for 2 weeks to 1 month until the liquid smells vinegary and tastes sour. The healthy bacteria that create vinegar require oxygen for the process, so it is important not to seal the container with a lid until the vinegar is as strong as you want it to be. When you think it's ready, use a funnel to pour it into glass bottles or large jars, cap or cork the bottle and store it away from direct heat or light.

TIP

To avoid a surprise explosion, burp your bottles of apple scrap vinegar by taking the top off to release any build-up of air over the next few days. The vinegar can be used for cooking or cleaning and will keep for up to one year.

SERVES 4

CHIPS

Master the art of making chips yourself – these are super crispy without any need for frying. Score.

3 large potatoes or 5 medium potatoes
oil
salt

Preheat the oven to 220°C.

Chop the potatoes into thick chip shapes by halving them, halving them again, then cutting then into wedges then strips.

Transfer them to a large baking tray, add a generous drizzle of oil and salt and pepper. Toss to coat, then make sure the chips are in a single layer making and aren't touching too much. This will help them crisp up and cook evenly.

Bake for 25–35 minutes, tossing/flipping at least once to ensure they cook evenly. Remove from the oven and serve immediately, tossing with more salt and pepper if liked.

MAKES ABOUT 500ML

PLANT-BASED MILK

Until the milkman – or woman – who comes to your door with fresh refillable glass bottles of plant milks is accessible to all, making your own from scratch at home is a fun and rewarding experience.

Some shop-bought milks are full of fillers so by making your own you know exactly know what you are putting into your body, and if you take the time to soak the base, it will taste sweeter than its pre-packaged counterparts.

CHOOSE A BASE
about 40g almonds, cashews, hazelnuts, pistachios, walnuts, oats, hemp or pumpkin seeds

+

ADD FRESH WATER
400ml

+

ADD A SWEETENER
2 tsp agave syrup, maple syrup, coconut sugar, brown sugar or 1 date

+

ADD A PINCH OF SALT

+

ADD A FLAVOUR (OPTIONAL)
pinch of ground turmeric, cinnamon, vanilla powder or cacao powder

Soak your chosen base in water from 30 minutes up to 4 hours (the longer you soak, the less time you'll need to blend the milk).

Drain, rinse and add to a high-speed blender. Add the water, sweetener and pinch of salt then blend on a high speed for 1–2 minutes. Add your additional flavour at this point, if wished, and blend again until smooth.

Pour the milk through a fine sieve or muslin and into a sterilised clean bottle. Keep in the fridge for up to 5 days.

TIP

There may be some pulp left over after straining. I use it in baking and and even make 'cheese' from this 'waste' but if you're looking to use yours, why not try my Oat pulp raspberry crumble on page 145.

MAKES ABOUT 180ML

DIY VANILLA EXTRACT

The one thing I dread having to buy in the supermarket? Vanilla extract. It's super-expensive and comes in a load of unnecessary packaging, but it's absolutely delicious. That's why I had to learn how to make my own, so that I never run out at an inconvenient time.

Homemade vanilla extract requires only two ingredients: vanilla pods and alcohol. I know that the pods are expensive, but this bulk will give you more bang for your buck. Great for baking, you'll wonder why you've never done this before.

3 vanilla pods
180ml bourbon, vodka, rum or whiskey

Make a cut down the length of the vanilla pods, but not all the way through them. Place the vanilla pods in a sealable jar and pour over your alcohol. Seal the jar and shake it every week – you want to make sure that there is occasional movement in the jar otherwise the pods will just float to the bottom and the fermentation won't occur evenly throughout the liquid. Repeat this step for about 2 months, then remove the pods and compost them.

Store the vanilla extract in a cupboard out of direct sunlight for up to a year.

SERVES 2

TURMERIC LEMON TONIC

Drinking regularly isn't necessarily conducive to a productive, mindful way of life. That's where this mocktail comes in. It gives you the feeling of having something alcoholic, without the hangover! Perfect when it's mid week and you have deadlines to hit and want something zingy and reviving.

- juice of 1 orange (use the peel – see pages 125 and 202–3)
- juice of 2 lemons (use the peel – see pages 125 and 202–3)
- 1 tbsp ginger, chopped or powder
- 1 tbsp turmeric, chopped or powder
- tonic water, to serve
- pinch of black pepper

If you have a juicer, go ahead and juice your orange, lemon, ginger and turmeric. If not, put the lemon and orange juice into a high-speed blender and blend the juice on high for 30 seconds.

Divide the juice between two glasses, top up with tonic water and add a pinch of freshly cracked black pepper.

If you end up juicing, save the pulp by placing into ice-cube trays and freezing. Add them to smoothies or use them to make dog biscuits (see page 201).

1 SERVING

RHUBARB GIN AND TONIC

2 tbsp Rhubarb syrup (see below)
40ml grapefruit juice
75ml gin
chilled tonic water
grapefruit peel and segments, to garnish

For the rhubarb syrup

2–3 rhubarb stalks, roughly chopped
185g caster sugar
230ml water

The first time I came into contact with rhubarb is when I was bartending at a well-known restaurant in New York City where they sliced it up and put it in a cocktail. I was quite taken with it.

I don't drink often, but when I do, my tipple of choice is a gin and tonic, so that's how I like to use this somewhat peculiar and sour vegetable.

Start by making the syrup. Put the chopped rhubarb, sugar and water into a saucepan and bring to a simmer over a medium heat. Cook until all the sugar has dissolved and the rhubarb is soft. Tranfer to a blender or food processor and purée on a high speed until smooth, then push through a sieve, allowing the clear syrup to collect underneath. Save the leftover pulp for your morning porridge or add to my Oat pulp raspberry crumble (see page 145). Store the syrup in a sealed sterilised bottle and chill in the fridge.

Fill a cocktail shaker with a handful of ice and add the rhubarb syrup, grapefruit juice and gin. Shake well and then strain into a glass filled with ice. Top with cold tonic water.

Garnish with a strip of grapefruit peel or segments and or thinly grated pieces of rhubarb. Cheers!

ZERO-WASTE HACKS

UPCYCLE THAT CAN

I'll be the first to say that I am not perfect. There are times where I don't have the ingredients or the access to create all my recipes on my own from scratch and then I see what I need in a can – staring at me. The positive thing about aluminum cans (as opposed to buying something in plastic) is that they're 100 per cent recyclable. They can be melted down and reformed without losing any quality, and the process can be repeated over and over again. If you do purchase a can, remember either to recycle it or repurpose it, using one of the following examples:

» Use it to store your pens, paintbrushes, or even cooking equipment like wooden spoons and spatulas

» Plant herbs or flowers in it: poke a few holes in the base, fill it with a layer of small stones, add a bit of soil and plant your seed. It will look beautiful by your kitchen windowsill.

DOGGY BISCUITS

Dogs got to eat too! These biscuits are made from pulp, but be sure to remove all seeds and err on the side of caution as some pet pooches can have very sensitive stomachs, so this one may not be for them!

If you don't have the equipment to make a cold-pressed juice at home, you can always ask the team at your local café for their leftover pulp. These biccies are perfect for human consumption too.

35g coconut oil
65g peanut butter
50g banana, mashed
120g oat flour, plus extra for dusting
about 130g almond pulp (from making your homemade nut milk see page 194)
about 70g carrot pulp
about 70g fruit or veggie pulp

Preheat your oven to 180°C.

Combine all the ingredients and mix well with a spoon. The mixture will be slightly wet but still thick and hold well. Scoop a tablespoon of mixture into your hand and roll using both your palms to form a ball. Place on a lightly floured baking tray and press the mixture softly to maintain a circular but flat shape. Bake for 30–40 minutes until firm and browned.

CANDIED CITRUS WASTE PEEL

Don't know what to do with you leftover citrus peel beside composting them? Here is another easy way to reduce waste in your kitchen (see also, page 125 for my Citrus bomb house cleaner). It's time to re-think what we 'throw away'. Before I automatically put potential food waste in the compost caddy, I take a moment and ask myself 'can I use this ingredient for anything else?' Most of the time, it's yes. Sprinkle your candied citrus peels on cereals, or pudding, like ice cream or cake.

2 grapefruit, 3 lemons. 4 oranges or 1 lime
270g caster sugar, plus 45g to coat

With a sharp knife, follow the curve of your fruit and cut the outermost peels leaving most of the white pith on fruit. Slice the peel lengthwise into 1cm-wide strips.

Bring 125ml of water to the boil in a small saucepan. Toss in the peel and cook until tender, about 10 minutes. Remove from the water and leave to dry on a wire rack.

Add the sugar to the same pot of water, bring to the boil and stir until the sugar dissolves. Add the peel and boil until they are translucent and you have a thick syrup, about 8–10 minutes. Transfer the peels to a wire rack, making sure they're not touching each other.

Leave the peel to dry for up to 1 hour, then transfer to a bowl and toss with 45g of sugar to coat. Any leftover sugar you can reuse again.

DRIED CITRUS SKIN

If you're overloading on citrus fruits at the moment and have made my Citrus bomb house cleaner or have candied the peel, then you probably need another use for those citrus skins. Drying them is a really simple way to preserve them and they make a great addition to any sweet or savoury dishes. Venetia recently made a big batch of granola and finished it off with dried citrus peel. If you haven't tried this before, I encourage you to stop what you are doing (not really, but really) and give use to that unwanted peel. Hello zing.

Preheat your oven to 90°C. Peel your citrus by removing only the skin. Be sure to leave the pith in contact with the fruit. Next, chop your peel into thin strips.

Place your peel on a baking sheet and bake in the oven for 15–20 minutes or until curled and slightly hardened.

Remove from the oven and leave to cool completely. Keep in a sealed and airtight container for up to 3 months in the fridge.

BANANA PEEL FERTILISER

If you're like me, I eat a lot of bananas, so I always have peels left afterwards. Like all plants, bananas contain important nutrients and can be planted in your back garden to help support plant and soil health. Recycling the peels back into your gardens returns essential nutrients to the soil where they can benefit other plants.

banana peels

Chop your banana peels into 2.5cm segments. By chopping them, you kickstart the compost process and release some of the beneficial vitamins and minerals in the peels. Dig holes about 15–30cm deep and plant your banana peels around your garden, preferably near other plants or trees to provide the most beneficial results.

06

21-DAY CHALLENGE

MORE PLANTS LESS WASTE 21-DAY CHALLENGE

We all need to start somewhere. No matter how small or big our change is, to create a better future we all need to do our part in protecting our only planet that we call home. This is my 21-day MORE PLANTS LESS WASTE challenge that will encourage and inspire you to create less waste and eat more plants in your everyday life. Why 21 days, you might ask? Because it takes 21 days to form a new habit. You can start at any time of the month, keep what you learn and inspire those around you to live more sustainably.

DAY 1: PLASTIC AUDIT

Create an audit of the rubbish you throw away. This gives you an idea of what you consume the most and gives you an opportunity to look for the alternative product such as a reusable water bottle for plastic water ones etc.

DAY 2: ASSEMBLE YOUR 'LESS WASTE TO GO' KIT

Get together the items you need when you're out and about. Maybe you already own them. Collect a reusable fork, knife, spoon, perhaps a metal straw and a reusable cloth/bandana as a napkin.

DAY 3: EAT WHAT YOU HAVE IN YOUR FRIDGE

We tend to buy more than we actually need. I love clearing out my fridge and cupboards and cooking what's in there.

DAY 4: SHOP LOCALLY FOR PRODUCE

Support your local producers. By doing so you reduce the amount of carbon emissions it took to bring your food to you.

DAY 5: FIGURE OUT YOUR COMPOST

Food that isn't composted and is chucked in a bin goes to landfill where it releases methane into our atmosphere and makes it harder for us to breathe. Turn back to page 58 to see my guide on how you can start composting – there are lots of different ways; through creating your own compost or using a general food waste bin from your local council.

DAY 6: GO BULK SHOPPING

If you can, go shopping for bulk ingredients and be sure to bring your bags/jars with you for refilling.

DAY 7: BUY VINTAGE

Fast fashion is one of the most polluting industries in the world. Shopping more at your local thrift or vintage shop is a less wasteful alternative.

DAY 8: NOURISH YOUR BODY

Most soap and shampoos come in plastic containers and are hard to recycle. Refill your soap and shampoos at a bulk shop or try making your own from scratch.

DAY 9: EAT MORE PLANTS

Devote today to eating only plants and natural whole foods – nothing processed.

DAY 10: DITCH PLASTIC WATER BOTTLES

To make this switch all you need to do is carry a reusable bottle with you wherever you go. You'll end up saving money too.

DAY 11: REPLACE KITCHEN PAPER

Ditch the kitchen paper because you don't need it. I reuse tea towels or old rags instead. While you're at it replace paper tissues with a handkerchief.

DAY 12: BRING YOUR CUP WITH YOU

Do you fancy a takeaway coffee or tea at your favourite cafe? Instead of using their disposable cups bring your own one with you to reduce the waste that ends up going to landfill.

DAY 13: BUY A MEAL IN YOUR REUSABLE CONTAINER

I challenge you to use your own container for your takeaway meal. It can sometimes feel nerve-wracking as this isn't quite the norm yet, but it feels great when you make it happen.

DAY 14: FERMENT

Fermenting foods is a great way to cut back on food waste. With a busy schedule, food often goes soft and spoiled in the blink of an eye. If you know you may not get a chance to cook that cabbage or carrot - consider pickling as it's a great shelf stabiliser.

DAY 15: MAKE A ZERO-WASTE BEAUTY PRODUCT

I have plenty of recipes in this book for you to create at home. Perhaps you fancy making a body scrub from leftover coffee grounds, or a ripe avocado face mask? I'm sure you'll be surprised by what you can create with less waste.

DAY 16: BUY BREAD IN A CLOTH BAG

Most bread we see in the supermarket is wrapped in plastic. Go straight up to the baker and ask for a fresh loaf and let them know you have your own bag with you too.

DAY 17: DO YOUR BIT!

Head out to the local park or beach and spend half an hour doing a plastic clean-up session. There are some amazing community initiatives across the country doing great things in this space every week that you can get involved in – it's both eye-opening and rewarding in equal measure.

DAY 18: TURN YOUR PHONE OFF

According to recent research, speaking on the phone for one hour a day can create the same carbon emissions as a flight from London to NYC. Try switching off for a day a week to reconnect with the world beyond your screen.

DAY 19: RECYCLE PROPERLY

Recycling is a whole big minefield in itself, but don't be discouraged. Set up your recycling bin with what you know can be recycled properly – drawing a diagram of what can and can't be recycled and pinning it up on your fridge is always helpful.

DAY 20: SAVE YOUR VEGGIE SCRAPS

Those food scraps you're about to throw away are not waste – that is veggie stock gold! Save your scraps to make stock (see page 176 for my recipe).

DAY 21: SHARE YOUR CHANGES AND CELEBRATE YOUR VICTORIES!

Let others know that you challenged yourself and made changes along the way. We all learn from one another and have a far better reach when we share our experiences. We even have the potential to inspire a community. It's the micro edits to our daily routines that hold the power for change!

Remember to celebrate and reward yourself – you've made it – even if you didn't achieve each goal. There is no perfection in this life and it's all about the journey. Enjoy your victory, take what you've learned and keep moving forward.

TAG ME ON YOUR #MOREPLANTSLESSWASTE JOURNEY

@MAXLAMANNA

A

B

C

D

E

F

G

H

I

J

K

L

M

N

O

P

Q

R

S

T

U

V

W

Y

Z

ACKNOWLEDGEMENTS

There are many people I need to thank who were a part of this journey and who have helped along the way to make this book truly special – you know who you are.

To the amazing dream team I had to make this book come to life. Thank you to OddBox who donated 'ugly' and wonky fruits and vegetables in the preparation of my recipes (no food was wasted in the process); to Andrew, for his amazing food photography; Ben, who captured my silly personality through video; Lou and Lara, who made my food look stunning; Imogen, who helped my writing and storytelling flow a lot better; and Abi, for the incredible design and layout.

Everyone at Yellow Kite who believed in my message and has made this book possible for the world to read. Thank you to Caitriona Horne and Rebecca Mundy, and a special thank you to Lauren Whelan who first approached and inspired me to spread my message wide and far.

To my agent Carly Cook, who believed in me and has calmed me down with many an English breakfast tea.

To all my friends who have encouraged me to keep going. Thank you Dad for your wisdom and for teaching me to enjoy the present moment. Thank you Mom for your love and kindness. My brother, Luke and sisters Gianne and Martia: thank you for your neverending support and love, even though I can be a pain of a brother sometimes.

To my Venetia, thank you for all that you do and your continuous love.

To all my readers, thank you so much. I'm so inspired by all of you.

METRIC/IMPERIAL CONVERSION CHART

All equivalents are rounded, for practical convenience.

Weight

25g	1 oz
50g	2 oz
100g	3½ oz
150g	5 oz
200g	7 oz
250g	9 oz
300g	10 oz
400g	14 oz
500g	1 lb 2 oz
1 kg	2¼ lb

Volume (liquids)

5ml		1 tsp
15ml		1 tbsp
30ml	1 fl oz	⅛ cup
60ml	2 fl oz	¼ cup
75ml		[1/3] cup
120ml	4 fl oz	½ cup
150ml	5 fl oz	[2/3] cup
175ml		¾ cup
250ml	8 fl oz	1 cup
1 litre	1 quart	4 cups

Length

1cm	½ inch
2.5cm	1 inch
20cm	8 inches
25cm	10 inches
30cm	12 inches

Volume (dry ingredients – an approximate guide)

butter	1 cup (2 sticks)	225g
rolled oats	1 cup	100g
fine powders *(e.g. flour)*	1 cup	125g
breadcrumbs (fresh)	1 cup	50g
breadcrumbs (dried)	1 cup	125g
nuts *(e.g. almonds)*	1 cup	125g
seeds (e.g. chia)	1 cup	160g
dried fruit *(e.g. raisins)*	1 cup	150g
dried legumes *(large, e.g. chickpeas)*	1 cup	170g
grains, granular goods and small dried legumes *(e.g. rice, quinoa, sugar, lentils)*	1 cup	200g
grated cheese	1 cup	100g

Oven temperatures

Celsius	Fahrenheit
140	275
150	300
160	325
180	350
190	375
200	400
220	425
230	450